J. H. (John Henry) Cornell, Wilhelm Langhans

The History of Music in Twelve Lectures

J. H. (John Henry) Cornell, Wilhelm Langhans

The History of Music in Twelve Lectures

ISBN/EAN: 9783337086527

Printed in Europe, USA, Canada, Australia, Japan

Cover: Foto ©Thomas Meinert / pixelio.de

More available books at **www.hansebooks.com**

THE HISTORY OF MUSIC

IN TWELVE LECTURES

BY

WILHELM LANGHANS.

TRANSLATED FROM THE GERMAN
(SECOND, ENLARGED EDITION, WITH ILLUSTRATIONS)

BY

J. H. CORNELL.

NEW YORK
G. SCHIRMER, 35 UNION SQUARE WEST SIDE.
1886.

AUTHOR'S PREFACE
TO THE SECOND EDITION.

The plan of these Lectures as also the grouping of the material are, notwithstanding considerable enlargement of the several sections, the same here as in the first edition and in the lectures, forming the basis of the book, delivered by me in 1877 and 1878 at Berlin. The chief aim that I then had in view was to awaken in larger circles an interest for music-history, and that by the examination not only of certain epochs lying closer to our intelligence but of its entire course of development. For proximately attaining this end in a limited time I had to content myself, as regards the representative characters of those epochs, with emphasizing in a general way their art-historical significance and referring to the excellent biographers that each of them has found in modern times: BACH in PHILIPP SPITTA, HANDEL in FRIEDRICH CHRYSANDER, GLUCK in ADOLPH BERNHARD MARX, HAYDN in CARL FERDINAND POHL, MOZART in OTTO JAHN, BEETHOVEN in ALEXANDER W. THAYER. With reference to more remote epochs I recommend to the reader, provided I have at all succeeded in instigating him through my scanty recital to a more exhaustive study, the valuable works of a FORKEL, an AMBROS and a FÉTIS; moreover, with special reference to the music of antiquity, the no less meritorious works of FRIEDRICH BELLERMANN, WESTPHAL, GEVAERT, WEITZMANN; to that of the Middle Age, of HEINRICH BELLERMANN, and of modern times, of FRANZ BRENDEL. But if any should deem the leap too great from my small monograph to those authors, treating their subject as they do with extreme profuseness to such the "Manual of music-history"

(Handbuch der Musikgeschichte) by A. von Dommer (2ᵈ edition, 1878, also his "Elements of Music" (Elemente der Musik) and revision of Koch's "Musical Lexicon" Musikalisches Lexicon) will afford a trustworthy basis for their study.

As to the scruples felt by some critics on account of my dragging the present time into the sphere of historical consideration — scruples that are at bottom well-founded, as I by no means deny — I judged that I might also in this edition disregard them, because the efforts of our prominent musical contemporaries almost entirely start out from historical premises, and we in profoundly occupying ourselves with them involuntarily direct our attention to the past. That Richard Wagner especially has, as writer and also as poet and musician, extensively contributed to enlivening the interest for the history of music, even the opponents of his art-tendency must concede, and I felt that even out of consideration for my knowledge I ought on this occasion not to overlook his labors as artist and esthetician. I do not by any means hold that the historian jeopardizes the objectivity necessary to him by retaining close contact with the development of his own time also; nay, I maintain even that he is bound never to lose sight of the relations between the "heretofore" and the "now", forasmuch as a great number of historical facts are comprehensible only in the light of the present. "It is the privilege of the living" — says Gustav Freytag in his "Pictures of German antiquity" (Bilder aus der deutschen Vergangenheit — "to interpret all the past according to the needs and claims of their own time. For the Monstrous and Inscrutable of historical life will be supportable to us only when we recognize in it a passing away corresponding to our reason and our heart's desire, in heaped up ruin an infinite source of new life, out of the Perishing the Becoming. Therefore a nation that rejoices in its Present loves also to recall its Past, because it recognizes in it the broadcast seed of its blooming fields."

Berlin, May, 1879.

W. LANGHANS.

TRANSLATOR'S PREFACE.

In editing the present work I have taken the liberty of occasionally omitting portions of it, in the interest of English-speaking readers and for giving the book a more generally popular character. These few omissions concern chiefly material of interest to Germans, as such, exclusively, also one or two explanations of a strictly scientific character, for which I have referred, instead, to easily accessible works in the English language. At the same time, not only has every single point of general interest been scrupulously retained, but considerable additions from approved sources have been made, with a view to greater copiousness or clearness where either seemed to me desirable.

New York, September, 1885.

J. H. CORNELL.

CONTENTS.

                                                                                           Page

I. **Antiquity.** Aim and plan of the study of music-history. — Characteristics of the music of the East-Indians, Chinese, Egyptians, Hebrews. — Music of the Greeks. — The ancient Tragedy. — Influence of Greek philosophy on art-development. — Lyrists instrumental virtuosos, theoreticians. — Decay of music under Roman dominion. — Emperor NERO . . . . 1—14

II. **The Music of the early Christian Age.** Dependence of early Christian art upon the antique. — Continued influence of Greek culture even after the migration of the nations. — THEODORIC, King of the Goths. — The Greek tonal-system as basis of the Christian. — Establishment of the first singing-schools at Rome. — Reforms instigated by Archbishop AMBROSE and Pope GREGORY. — Charlemagne. — The Singing-school of St. Gall . . 15—25

III. **The Beginnings of Polyphonic Music.** The Arabians and the Northern nations. — Musical instruments and the "Organum". — HUCBALD. — Neumes. — GUIDO D'AREZZO. — Solmisation. — Mensural music. — FRANCO OF COLOGNE. — Scholastic philosophy 26—39

IV. **The Musical Sovereignty of the Netherlanders.** Crusades. — Troubadours. — Minnesingers and Mastersingers. — Guilds of instrumental musicians. — German Folk-song. — The Papacy in Avignon. — Discant. — The Netherlanders in Rome: DUFAY. OCKENHEIM, JOSQUIN. — Improvements in the art of music-printing. — Preparation for the Renascence by DANTE, PETRARCH BOCCACCIO . . . . 40—53

V. **Luther's Reformation and the Renascence.** Plastic art and music at the beginning of the 16th century. — Protestant church-song. — Its re-action on Catholic church-music. — PALESTRINA. — Classic art. — Attempts at resuscitating antique art. — Monody and recitative. — CACCINI and PERI. — The Opera . 54—62

VI. **Italian opera.** Venice. — WILLAERT gives the church-music of Venice a dramatic character. — His pupil ZARLINO introduces the pure diatonic system. — A. and J. GABRIELI. — Development of the Opera. — MONTEVERDE. CAVALLI. — Chamber-music style. — The Neapolitan School of A. SCARLATTI. — Its propagation throughout Europe. — Artistic singing. — Rivalry of

		Page
	the later Neapolitans with GLUCK and MOZART. — ROSSINI. — VERDI	63—74
VII.	**French Opera.** PERRIN and CAMBERT, founders of the national opera in France. — Development of the latter by LULLI and RAMEAU. — Equal temperament. — Comic opera. — Bouffonites and Anti-bouffonites. — The Philosophy of Enlightenment of the 18th century. — JEAN JACQUES ROUSSEAU. — GLUCK. — The Paris Conservatory of Music. — Foreign composers in the service of French opera: CHERUBINI, SPONTINI, MEYERBEER	75—91
VIII.	**German opera.** First operatic performance in Germany. — Rise of a German national opera in Hamburg. — REINHARD KEISER. — Ennobling of the Song-play by J. A. HILLER. — DITTERSDORF and Comic Opera. — MOZART's "Entführung" and "Zauberflöte". — BEETHOVEN's "Fidelio"	92—103
IX.	**The Oratorio.** Passion and Mysteries in the Middle Age. — The musical congregations of PHILIP NERI. — Introduction of the dramatic style into the church: CAVALIERE, VIADANA, CARISSIMI. — LOTTI, CALDARA, MARCELLO, the last representatives of the Venetian School. — Development of church-music in Germany: ORLANDUS LASSUS, ECCARD, HANS LEO HASLER, HEINRICH SCHÜTZ. — Mixture of operatic and church styles in Hamburg. — Passion-text of the licentiate Brockes. — HANDEL and BACH. — Development of musical affairs in England. — MENDELSSOHN, and his "St. Paul" and "Elijah" . .	104—121
X.	**Instrumental Music.** The Organ, and keyed string-instruments. — The Lute. — Tablature. — Bow-instruments and wind-instruments. — Instrumental style. — Instrumental music-forms. — Cyclical forms: Partita, Suite, Sonata. — The modern pianoforte sonata and the orchestral symphony. — German philosophy of the 18th century	122—140
XI.	**The Romanticists of the 19th century.** Influence of romanticism on lyric poetry. — Folk-song and art-song. — Development of the latter by FRANZ SCHUBERT and ROBERT FRANZ. — Romantic opera: SPOHR, WEBER, MARSCHNER. — Romantic instrumental music: MENDELSSOHN, SCHUMANN. — Songs without words. — French romanticists: BERLIOZ, LISZT, CHOPIN. — Program-music. — Modern pianoforte-playing	141—156
XII.	**Richard Wagner**	157—173

APPENDIX.

Table for memorizing certain dates of musico-historical importance		175—178
INDEX		179—185

I.
ANTIQUITY.

To appreciate rightly and enjoy fully the works of the human mind, we must not only thoroughly study these works themselves, but also be acquainted with the conditions under which they could and had to attain to maturity. If then it may be maintained that we cannot be successfully occupied with the arts and sciences unless we study at the same time the historical course of their development, this is especially true in regard of Music. This is justly called the most subjective among the arts, for, in view of the incorporeity of its material, the quickly passing tone, and in the absence of a prototype and corrective such as the other arts possess in the visible world surrounding us, it seems impossible to estimate the value of a musical art-work according to fixed rules; and in fact, diversity of opinion within this sphere is not infrequently so wide, that what at one time and in one place is considered beautiful, other times and other men reject as ugly. To acquire therefore a solid foundation for musical judgment the study of history is the only sure way, such a study, that is, as does not content itself with simply taking cognizance of historical facts, but seeks to recognize these in their inter-connexion as effects of general principles. Thus considered, even the seemingly barren epochs of music-history will acquire significance, the efforts of former generations will awaken sympathy, even when they were not crowned with immediate success, and to both the past and the onward-pressing present, though their aims may not yet be clear to us, we shall bring a better understanding than would be the case without that assistance.

In occupying ourselves with music-history we must, however, if it is to be really profitable to us, not confine ourselves to certain epochs corresponding to the sensationary method*) peculiar to the present time. In the development of music there are no leaps: indeed, it can be said that here the connexion of the various epochs of history is more intimate than in the other departments of mental culture. Not even the deep gap between the ancient and the modern world availed to abolish this connexion, for the music-forms of the Greeks passed over almost unchanged into the post-christian music, and formed, as will be shown more at length farther on, the basis of the Roman churchsong, upon which, again, at a later period the mighty edifice of modern music could lift itself up.

But even in still more remote times, among the oldest civilized nations of the ancient world, manifold points present themselves in which their view of music joins hands with that of the more modern nations — reason enough why we should not pass over those earliest culture-epochs in perfect silence, as sometimes is done in musico-historical works of smaller compass. Through all antiquity runs the belief in the divine origin of music and in its capacity to work miracles. Among the **East-Indians** Brahma himself is held to be the creator of music, and his son Nared the inventor of the national musical instrument, the guitarlike Vina, just as among the Greeks the origin of the lyre was traced to Hermes, and among the Egyptians to the god Thaut. If, according to the Greek legend, an Orpheus and an Amphion by means of song tamed wild beasts and built cities, if the trumpets of the Israelites had power to overthrow the walls of Jericho, in the same way, certain melodies of the East-Indians caused him who sang them to be consumed by fire, others had the power of eclipsing the sun, others, again, produced rain, of which latter kind one, on the occasion of a drought in the ricefields of Bengal, delivered the people from a famine.

The music-systems established by the East-Indian scholars exhibit also agreement in many points with those of the other cultured peoples of antiquity. To none of them, the eminently gifted Greeks not excepted, was it granted to discover that which to the modern ear sounds so natural — the division of the Octave

---

* German, Empfindungsweise, meaning the manner of receiving — way one is affected by — the impressions made on the soul through the senses, such as the sight, hearing, etc.   *Translator.*

into twelve half-steps. Like the Greek music-theory, the East-Indian also had the quarter-step, and even still finer tone-differences, and, conformably to the variety of the intervals, a great number of keys, of which the musicologist SOMA names no less than nine hundred and sixty. Just here, however, be it observed that the idea of "key" in antiquity was different from the modern one, and comprehended more: the scales of those keys — which latter should more properly be called "tone-combinations" or "melodies" — are determined partly by the starting of the octave-series from different degrees of the same scale (thus, *e. g.*, from the tones of the *C*-major scale, sung from *D* to *d*, again from *E* to *e* etc., but without any chromatic signs, six new scales arise, each having its own peculiar order of intervals), partly by the modification of individual intervals by raising or lowering, partly by overleaping certain degrees of the scale. If the acuteness of the Greeks availed to reduce the multitude of variants originating in this way to an easily intelligible system, the exuberant mind of the Orientals was unable to distinguish the essential from the accidental, and to discover a universal law underlying the countless tone-combinations.

In strong contrast with the unbridled fantasticism of the East-Indians is the rationalistically sober nature of the **Chinese**. Qualified as they are for all labors in which success depends upon unremitting industry and attention, yet their performance in those departments in which imagination and mental elevation turn the scale are only of subordinate value. Accordingly, neither could music exercise with them that elevating and inspiring effect as with the Orientals, though this did not prevent its being highly prized as a subject of scientific study and also as a means of educating youth. In the latter respect China shows itself in accord with Greece. "If you would know" — so runs a saying of the first of the Chinese philosophers, CONFUCIUS (500 years before Christ — "whether a country is well governed and of good morals, listen to its music". But we find the same opinion repeatedly expressed by PLATO and ARISTOTLE: in another point, too, the philosophers of Greece agree with those of China, viz., in that they ascribe to certain tone-successions a special fitness for educating and ennobling the young, and put them for this reason under the protection of the laws. — The musical system of the Chinese differs from that of the East-Indians chiefly by its meagerness: if the latter revelled in a multitude of intervals so small that they would not be recognizable by the modern ear, the Chinese went to the other extreme: to them even the diatonic scale is not simple enough, they go farther and deprive it of two of its tones — the Fourth and the Seventh. But here again is seen an analogy of the Chinese with the Greek music, for that scale of the Chinese, *c d e g a c* — which C. M. VON WEBER also has made the basis of his overture to "Turandot" — finds its counterpart in that of OLYMPUS[*], who, as ARISTOXENUS relates, omitted in the minor scale the fourth and seventh degrees, and, admiring and adopting the scale constructed after this analogy, composed in it melodies of the Doric key.[**] Moreover, the effort to interrupt the strict diatonic series may be traced even down to the latest times: at this very day that scale with fourth and seventh lacking survives in the national airs of the Scotch, and the minor scale of the Gypsies, which has been made known through LISZT's "Hungarian Rhapsodies", follows, with its twice occurring augmented second, the same principle.

The obstinate adherence to the traditional, which kept the intellectual life of the Chinese spell-bound and deprived them of the fruits of a culture a thousand years old, hindered them also from farther perfecting their music: even Prince TSAY-YU, so universally esteemed as music-connoisseur, could not succeed in having the two lacking half-steps admitted into the above-described scale of five degrees: to intrude these tones into the scale, said his opponents, was the same as to add to the hand a sixth and seventh finger. It was for the same reason that the **Egyptians,** who were, artistically, incomparably more richly gifted, were obliged to stop half-way in the career of their mental development. The high rank that they held for the time being among the civilized peoples of antiquity is attested by the artistic worth

---

[*] A famous musician of Phrygia, of whom PLUTARCH says that he was the first to introduce among the Greeks the knowledge of stringed instruments; PLATO, that his music inflamed his auditors; ARISTOTLE, that it exalted the soul; and PLUTARCH, that it surpassed in simplicity all other music.
Translator.

[**] As we also learn from ARISTOXENUS, Olympus was on this account reckoned the inventor of the enharmonic tone-genus, of which mention will be made farther on. p. 20.

of their numerous monuments which have been preserved to posterity, as also by the influence that they exercised upon the scientific and artistic culture of the nations around them, as, for instance, when the most celebrated investigators of Greece, a PYTHAGORAS, a HERODOTUS, and, as late as the fourth century before Christ, a PLATO, did not shrink from the voyage across the sea in order to have a share in the Egyptian philosophies. It is true that at PLATO's time mental activity among the Egyptians seems to have come to a halt, as we may conclude from the following passage in the second book of his "Laws": "Is it allowed" (he asks) "that everything which to a poet appears beautiful in a poem or a song, should also be taught to the young? This is allowed everywhere except in Egypt. — But why is this not allowed in Egypt? — This is indeed to be wondered at. To the Egyptians, however, it had long been known that the young in the cities should be accustomed only to beautiful forms and to good music; but what should be the nature of the beautiful forms and good music is determined by their priests, and to neither painters nor musicians nor other artists is it permitted to introduce anything new, differing from those patterns which have been once recognized as beautiful. Thence it comes also that their paintings and statues which were executed ten thousand years ago are in not a single point better or worse than those which are made at the present day". But with this the death-sentence of the arts was pronounced: for, as soon as it is forbidden to surpass the ancients, to enlarge the boundaries of art and give sanction to new laws, self-evidently the creative faculty must become extinct and intellectual stagnation must take its place. That notwithstanding all this, music occupied an important place in the public and private life of the Egyptians, is shown by the figurative representations, which have been discovered in the royal sepulchres and on other monuments, of singers and instrumentalists, now individually, now united in choirs and orchestras, as also by the variety of the instruments there depicted, among which the many-stringed harp appears oftenest and gives proof of the luxuriant, pompous character of the music. Yet all endeavors to enrich music outwardly afford no compensation for the lack of interior productiveness. In the history of music Egypt may take only a subordinate position compared with the Hebrews and Greeks, the two nations of antiquity which, to be sure, received from the Egyptians the impulse to intellectual activity, but by their own strength were soon to far surpass their pattern in one way or another.

The influence exercised by Egypt on *Grecian* culture is especially clearly noticeable in the works of fine art of the earliest development-period of Greece, as for example in the so-called Apollo of Tenea, which exhibits outright the Egyptian type. Still more important must have been this influence on the culture of the *Jewish* nation, whose ancestors had as poor nomads taken refuge among the Egyptians, and were compelled to dwell with them for centuries in a condition of dependence. During the short national independence which the Hebrews enjoyed afterwards, there was developed among them also a peculiar art whose significance for the public worship as also for the social life is unmistakably evidenced by the countless statements referring thereto in the Old Testament. This temporary upward flight was, however, followed by centuries of political dependence upon nations of a comparatively high civilization, during which time the artistic acquisitions of that short epoch of freedom were of necessity gradually lost, till at length Greek culture, overflowing everything, impressed its seal upon Judaism also. Certainly, the Hebrews have cultivated one side of their nature with a consistency which is rare in the history of nations: their attention rather to the inner man than to the exterior life, and the consequent purer and higher theory of life which steadfastly resisted all the hostile influences of the surrounding peoples, — these sufficiently attest the peculiarity of the Jewish national spirit and account for the interest which has in all ages been taken in the history of its development. But it is precisely these peculiarities of the Hebrews that must raise doubt as to the artistic endowment of the latter: moreover, a study in detail of the ancient Hebrew music cannot be remunerative, for the very reason that concerning the nature of the latter as good as nothing has been communicated to us by contemporary writers, and besides, of monuments, such as give information of the history of other peoples, there is in the Jewish country an utter lack.*

* As the only monument of Jewish antiquity we may regard the relief in the interior of the triumphal arch of Titus, at Rome, in which, in the pro-

If, accordingly, we may obtain a somewhat clear idea of the Hebrew music only mediately, through the study of Egyptian and Babylonian antiquities, we have immediate and copious information concerning the music of the Greeks, in their writings and monuments. Under far more favorable conditions than in the case of the Hebrews they could undertake to develop according to the national taste the elements of the arts and sciences, handed down by the Egyptians. Their teachable nature was assisted by the geographical situation of their country: the facility of maritime intercourse induced them at an early period to open communications, with a view to the exchange of material and intellectual goods, with the seaboard peoples of the Mediterranean, to some extent their superiors in culture. This intercourse was also to conduce to the development of their musical faculties: the impulse to theoretical speculation they received chiefly from Egypt, where even in the remotest antiquity music was cultivated in connexion with mathematical and astronomical investigations; their practical music, on the other hand, was influenced prëeminently by the connexions with Asia Minor, for from this country Greece received, with the grape-culture and the Bacchus-worship, also the wildly passionate music belonging to it, accompanied as it was with shrill and far-sounding wind-instruments. This music being blended with the indigenous music, arranged according to strict proportion, the cooperation of their heterogeneous elements called into existence that national music of whose elevating power the ancient writers give testimony in many places, and which attained its highest effect in tragedy.

If we accept WESTPHAL's* opinion as the correct one, according to which in the *ancient tragedy* not only the choruses but also the monologues and dialogues were recited musically, and it at all events "approached more closely to our modern opera than to our reciting drama", this art-species may rightfully claim the special attention of the music-historian. The story of its development is sketched in a few words. It takes its origin, according to the statement of DROYSEN (in his "Didaskalien zum

cession of Jewish captives, among other sacred treasures of the Temple of Jerusalem is carried also the metal wind-instrument of the Jews, mentioned in the Old Testament under the name of SCHOFAR or KEREN.

* RUDOLPH WESTPHAL, Greek Rhythmics and Harmonics.

"Aischylos" from the festivals celebrated at the time of the vintage in honor of Bacchus, at which, amid impassioned songs a goat was offered to the god.* Choruses and dancing of the participants of the festival disguised as satyrs, whose leader recited in song during the pauses the sufferings of the god, formed the principal element of these rural festivals, which with the advancement of civilization attracted the attention of the cities also, and soon assumed an artistic form. THESPIS (about 600 B. C.) was the first to infuse into them the dramatic element, by bringing the narrator into a determinate relation to the chorus; he likewise regulated the movements of the chorus and gave it a costume corresponding to the subject of the action. If these artistic innovations of THESPIS found, on the one hand, violent adversaries, for example in the law-giver SOLON, yet the great public seems to have recognized his efforts, as we may conclude from his art-tours, on which he is said to have carried his properties with him on a cart — that Thespis-cart, the memory of which, as symbol of a travelling troupe of players, is preserved to this day.

A series of advances was still necessary before Tragedy arrived at that degree of exterior and interior perfection in which we find it at the time of AESCHYLUS. But all the improvements that it experienced during those years of development, the perfecting of the arts of dancing and gesture, the introduction of a second actor and herewith of dialogue, the use of the mask and the buskin, which seemed necessary for making the outward show harmonize with the majestic representations that people made to themselves of the heroes, — all this does not suffice to explain the powerful effect that AESCHYLUS' tragedy produced on the minds of the Greeks. This effect had its real cause rather in the national upsoaring of Greece resulting from the heroic prosecution of the Persian wars, as also in the deeply religious sensationary method of the Grecian people who at that time had not yet forgotten the original significance of tragedy as an act of divine worship. The philosophy of that age, whose aim was the investigation of divine things, the poetic strain in which it set forth its doctrines, nourished the enthusiasm of the people for the lofty and sublime,

---

* The Greek word for "tragedy" — *Tragodia* — is compounded from "Tragos" a goat, and "Ode" a song, hence signifies literally "song at the sacrifice of the goat."

and just as poetizing and thinking (reasoning), the diametrical opposites among the mental activities,* met in the works of the philosophers, so also in the dramas of AESCHYLUS. If, moreover, it be remembered that he himself repeatedly staked his life on the battle-field for the honor of his native land, it is not difficult to understand the severity of his ethical conceptions, his firm adherence to the poet's mission "to teach the citizens virtue and right". So little as the prophets of Israel their powerful exhortations — observes DROYSEN — did he compose his dramas for mere æsthetic reasons. They were to him sermons to his people, and only in this view have the seriousness of his thoughts, the gloomy magnificence of his language, the deeply passionate repose of his theory of life, their whole power.

It was necessary to sketch a picture of the *poet* AESCHYLUS, in order to form an idea of his merits as *musician*, since as regards the latter point nothing more is known than that he was also the musical composer of his dramas, as, generally speaking, antiquity applies the word "poet" poietes, to him only who combines in his person the poet and the musician. Concerning the nature of his music we can speak by way of conjecture only, yet we may assume with some certainty that in strict adhesion to the rhythm of the verse it was like our recitative or the chant of the Roman liturgy, whose formulas are modelled after the cadence of ordinary speech and are rooted in primeval traditions. If, accordingly, the music of AESCHYLUS' tragedy is hardly to be compared, in point of variety and absoluteness, with the modern music, this defect of the tone-language was doubtless counterbalanced by wealth of musical elements in the spoken language**

---

* "The object of Poetry", — says Lord BULWER, in his translation of SCHILLER'S Poems and Ballads — "differing essentially from that of abstract Wisdom, is not directly to address the reasoning faculty — but insensibly to rouse it through the popular medium of the emotions. * * * * The fault of" certain of SCHILLER'S poems which he names "is, that they strain too much the faculty with which Poetry has least to do, viz., the mere reason", etc.
Translator.

** By musical elements of speech are meant the so-called *onomato-poetic* words, *i. e.*, such as indicate their meaning by their sound alone, as, *ding-dong*, *thunder*, *cuckoo*, *buzz*, *howl*, *hiss*, *tick-tack* etc., in distinction to those whose meaning is conventional and which become intelligible to us only through education, as is the case with all words not included in the species in its then stage of development). It may even be assumed that the artistic effect of AESCHYLUS' dramas is chiefly due to the equilibrium that prevailed between the language of emotions and that of ideas, between tone and speech, a relation that is possible only at a time when neither one nor the other is yet compelled by the degree of its development to follow special paths.

This relation of equilibrium was, however, not to exist long. As early as SOPHOCLES' time the "gloomy magnificence" of AESCHYLUS' poetry gives way to a clearer, more determinate manner of expression, but EURIPIDES exhibits himself so predominantly as word-poet that we can easily understand his determination to leave the musical setting of his tragedies to another, a musician by profession. In intimate connexion with this poetico-musical transformation is the tendency, inaugurated about the middle of the 5th century B. C., of the Grecian philosophy. The now generally accepted *Sophistic philosophy* no longer — unlike the previous schools — regards the universe, generally and collectively, but *man*, considered in himself alone, as the worthiest object of investigation; but in order to fathom the human soul a suitable language is the first requisite, and the cultivation of such a one, as also of grammar, of the art of consistent thinking and of oral interchange of thought of logic and of dialectics) was of necessity a matter of primary importance to the disciples of sophistic phi-

---

first mentioned. The history of the development of language shows how, with the progress of that development, the former element was more and more supplanted by the second. "At the beginning" says R. WAGNER Collective Writings and Poems, article "Music of the Future", "the formation of the conception of an object was almost identical with the subjective sensation of it, and the assumption that the first human language must have been very similar to song would perhaps not seem ridiculous. From a signification of words which was felt in a manner in any case altogether sensuously subjective, human language evolved itself in a more and more abstract sense, in such a way that finally but a merely conventional meaning of the words remained, which deprived sensation of any share in understanding them, while at the same time their construction was made utterly dependent on rules which had to be learned." It need not be proved, that a language that has reached such a stage of development and is, so to speak, half torpid, is incomparably less favorable to the flight of poetic fancy than in the condition of youthful flexibility, and that the revivification of the "musical" elements that have been lost to language, must be for poetry, especially when intended to be joined with music, of very great advantage. Compare Chap. VII of this work.)

losophy. These endeavors had the twofold result of promoting knowledge and of rendering more and more intimate the relations of man to man. On the other hand, it is not without good grounds that the predicate "sophistical" is at the present day applied in a reproachful sense only; for as mastery in these arts of logic and rhetoric became greater and greater, virtuosity was made the chief thing among the sophists, to that degree that language had to serve less frequently for the investigation of truth than for dialectic sham fights. To what extent eloquence had at this time become an end to itself is shown by the fact that one of those virtuosos of oratory undertook on his art-travels to speak, in two discourses in immediate succession, once *for*, the second time *against* one and the same thing.

In consequence of this catastrophe music could no longer retain the high place it had till then taken in the life of the Greeks. Language no longer needed, for the aims it now pursued, the cooperation of musical tone. But meanwhile in the domain of music a similar process of development had been gone through: a new species of poetry, called, after the instrument used by the poet for accompanying his recitation, *lyric*, had attained among the Greeks, especially the Ionians inhabiting the coast of Asia Minor, a high degree of cultivation. In contradistinction to the choral songs, which express the sentiments of a universality, in the poems of the Ionian lyrist, of an *Arion*, a *Sappho*, an *Anacreon*, the individual sentiments, the moods of the multifariously agitated particular soul attain to artistic representation. Here music could and had to play an incomparably more important part than in the other species of poetry, here it was seen to be, in the faculty of expressing the most secret emotions of the soul, superior to spoken language. And, just as language, with its ever increasing power of expression, could dispense with the association of music, so also music now began to withdraw from words, to follow thenceforth its own way, — according to HERDER's expression "a dangerous separation for the defenceless human race: for music without words transplants us into a realm of obscure ideas: it awakens, in each one after its fashion, feelings slumbering in the heart, which in the torrent or the tide of artificial tones without words find no guide or leader" (*Zur schönen Literatur und Kunst*, Part XVI, p. 33). From this time forward instrumental music developed itself as a particular species: lyre and "aulos" — the latter generally anglicised as "flute", but in form and tone more closely corresponding to our clarinet or oboe — appear as solo-instruments in the musaic contests, and in one of the Pythian games instrumental virtuosity, in the person of the flutist SAKADAS who even undertook to represent in tones Apollo's fight with the serpent, celebrates a brilliant triumph.

To account fully for the short duration of the palmy days of Greek art we must once more refer to the effects of the sophistic philosophy and its principles. closely allied as they were to scepticism. "Man is the measure of all things. As any thing seems to any one, so it is for him. Only relative truth exists. The existence of the gods is uncertain" — such is the assertion of one of its chiefs. PROTAGORAS: but nothing could be more inimical to artistic enthusiasm than the axiomatic tendency to doubt that is here expressed; in a special manner the esteem for tragedy. which, conformably to its origin, was regarded as an act of divine worship, must have decreased in proportion as the religious belief of the people was shaken. After the leadership in Greece had, upon the close of the Peloponnesian war (B. C. 404), been transferred from Athens to Sparta, the art-creative faculty of the Grecian people gradually died out, and became totally extinct coincidently with the loss of the national independence resulting from the victory of Philip of Macedon at Chaeronea (B. C. 328). The preservation of that which previous generations had created now becomes the mission of the Grecian mind: making poetry gives way to speculative thought, artistic practice to theory and the structure of systems. Musical theory also finds its representatives, the most prominent of whom was ARISTOXENUS, surnamed "the musician", the first one to recognize the *hearing* as the sole criterion of tone-relationships, in opposition to the school of PYTHAGORAS, which, as in everything else so also in music, made *number* exclusively the regulating principle. Of the music-systems which then arose we shall give farther on, in passing over to speak of the modern music, begotten of those systems, the most important details; at present we will close our survey of the musical achievements of antiquity with the *Roman empire*.

If it was the mission of Greece, as antitype and teacher to show the world the way — as ISOCRATES the orator once expresses himself — the aim of the Romans was, before everything else, to win and consolidate material dominion. It was, accordingly, above all things practical and political problems whose solution was to occupy them, the artistic ones could not, along side of the others, find any consideration. And when at length they had accomplished their supreme end, the sovereignty over all the nations of the earth which were known to them, it was now too late to make up for what they had neglected in the domain of ideas: Rome had at all times to be content to satisfy its artistic requirements by borrowing from friendly nations, especially from Greece. This was in fact done at the time of the emperors on a magnificent scale: just as the globe was pillaged in order to heap up the works of plastic art of all schools and all lands in the public squares and the palaces of Rome, so too the city became a rallying-point of the musicians also of all the nations subject to the empire. The feeling for massive effects appears to have been predominant among the musical public of Rome, for as early as JULIUS CESAR's time SUETONIUS narrates that once during a public solemnity twelve thousand male and female singers and players sojourned in the city; and HORACE complains at the time of AUGUSTUS "that the modest flute with few holes, which satisfied the fathers, was forced, on account of the great dimensions of the playhouses of his time, to give way to noisy instruments."

If this musical tendency, whose aim was powerful effect, can in no wise awaken our interest, it must excite downright disgust to see art dragged through the mire as it was under the emperor NERO, who had, as is well known, among other hallucinations that of publicly figuring as virtuoso in singing and on the harp. His voice was so unmusical and his delivery so abominable, that on his first appearance (A. D. 60) the listeners knew not whether to laugh or to weep, and it was only by the help of a well-organised claque that the expressions of displeasure could be smothered. He afterwards undertook an art-journey to Greece, where he caused himself to be crowned with every prize that he could in any way lay his hands on, without meeting with any opposition whatever — a sad evidence of the demoralization that had invaded this soil which had once been consecrated by the muses. Soon after this, however, NERO's fantastic artist-career was to come to an end. In the year 60, A. D., GALBA was proclaimed emperor.

and nothing remained for NERO but to take his own life, at the age of thirty — a life which disgraced not only him but also his contemporaries, whose servility not even their artistic conscience kept within limits.

Under such circumstances it could be only a gain for humanity that the torch of the ancient civilization, that had so long lightened the world, was at length extinguished, when the Roman colossus at the first impact of the barbarians bursting in from the North fell in ruins. The bright light radiated from Greece had, it is true, to be followed for a century long by darkness, yet during this period of seeming stagnation a new spirit and new forms were to attain their development, and most especially with reference to music we may apply in this case the words of SCHILLER:

"The Ancient, crumbling, falls; the times are changed;
And new life blooms and springs up from the ruins."

II.

THE MUSIC OF THE EARLY CHRISTIAN AGE.

The mighty revolution that with the introduction and propagation of Christianity took place in all the domains of the intellectual life, necessarily brought with it in its train a fundamental change in art-theories also. Yet here the new spirit is manifested at first with diffidence only: just as Greece had in the infantile stage of its artistic development most closely followed Egypt, so now the early Christian civilization leans upon that of the Greeks. In this epoch also it is plastic art that affords us the positive evidence of the absolute dependence of the younger upon the elder civilization; the paintings in the Roman catacombs, in which the early Christians met for purposes of divine worship, exhibit everywhere the familiar figures and situations of the ancient mythology and fable applied to the illustration of biblical events: Orpheus, taming wild beasts, answers with slight modification for Daniel in the lions' den; Hermes carrying the goat, a type often reproduced by the Greek artists, for the Good Shepherd carrying home the stray lamb on his shoulders; Jonah and the whale that spat him out are scarcely distinguishable from Arion and his dolphin. To assume a higher degree of independence in the *music* of the first Christians would be in no wise justifiable: the testimonies of contemporary writers afford, in the absence of musical documents of that period, ample proofs of the contrary. For, if PLINY the younger relates of the Christian congregations of his time "that they sing to Christ, as to a god, an antiphonal hymn", and the Jewish scholar PHILO, residing at Alexandria, says of the Therapeutæ and Essenes, two sects converted to Christianity by the Apostles themselves, that they accompanied their

liturgical song with religious gestures, with steps forward and
backward, all this points to an immediate connexion with the
music and mimic art of the Greek tragedy. It may perhaps be
assumed that from the beginning of the Christian era it was the
earnest desire of the disciples of the new religion to simplify the
Greek music, which had become more and more voluptuous —
one of the earliest of the fathers of the Church, CLEMENT OF AL-
EXANDRIA towards the end of the 2d century), on this account for-
bade the members of his congregation the use of the chromatic
tone-series in the music of the church, — on the whole, however,
it may be conjectured that the chant of the first Christians,
though filled with a new spirit, was nevertheless as to its form
a faithful copy of the ancient music.

Nor did the introduction of Christianity as state religion
under Constantine the Great, A. D. 333, avail to bring about a
sudden change in the musical situation; even under the political
conditions which the migration of nations (A. D. 375) had totally
altered, the power of Greek civilization appears yet unbroken
That the time was not yet come to exchange it for another the
so-called barbarians may very likely have felt; for with few exceptions they were by no means wanting in reverence for the
civilization of the old world; as also they are on the whole to
be held far less answerable for the ravages and devastations committed at that time than the Romans, demoralized by centuries
of corruption, among whom avarice and frivolity had stifled every
feeling of veneration for their glorious past. But of all the peoples
that about the middle of the first Christian century overran Italy,
the **Goths**, as being indisputably the most gifted among them,
deserve the most esteem; especially did the reign of their king
THEODORIC died A. D. 520 in those days of wild ferment exert a
wholesome influence on the reorganization of affairs. In the
history of music likewise his name deserves to be mentioned: at
his court resided the musicographers, BOETHIUS and CASSIODORUS,
the last scientific representatives of antiquity; the former highly
esteemed even up to the end of the Middle Age as a musical
authority, although he made his appearance only as translator and
expounder of the older Greek music; the other, CASSIODORUS, to
be reckoned among Christian authors, in so far at least as he
was converted in old age to Christianity. That the fame of

THEODORIC as a connoisseur of art extended far beyond the borders of his kingdom is evidenced — not to give other proofs — by the petition addressed to him by the Frankish king CLOVIS to send him a citherode* who might domesticate in his country also the art — so greatly flourishing in Italy — of singing to the accompaniment of the cithara. It was BOËTHIUS who received from THEODORIC, with the most flattering compliments, the commission to select the artists most fitted for that purpose.

With BOËTHIUS, who afterwards fell into disgrace with his king, and, being accused of participation in a conspiracy of the Roman national party against the Gothic rule, was executed (A. D. 524) at Pavia, the mission of antiquity in respect to the progress of civilization had come to an end. But before turning to the musical reconstructions now inaugurated, let us make brief mention of the *Greek music-system*, on which they are based. The foundation of this system is not, as with the moderns, the eight-tone series, or Octave, but a series of four tones in the compass of a minor** Fourth, the *Tetrachord*, whose origin is to be traced to the four-stringed lyre. The Tetrachord, which invariably includes two progressions of a step*** and one of a half-step,† is differently named according to the relative position of this half-step, viz: *Doric* (when the latter is at the bottom, as: $\widehat{ef} — g — a$), *Phrygian* (when in the middle, as: $d — \widehat{ef} — g$), or *Lydian* (when at the top, as: $c — d — \widehat{ef}$). From the junction of two tetrachords of the same species arise the (respectively Doric, Phrygian, Lydian) *Octave-species* (Harmonia) —

DORIC.

---

* From the Greek *Kitharodos*, one who accompanies his singing by playing on the *cithara*, a stringed instrument most resembling the guitar.
Translator.

** The word "minor" is here used preferably to, and as identical with, the old-fashioned expression "perfect" to which corresponds the word "rein" in the German original. See my *Primer of Modern Tonality*, 3d edition, *Note*, p. 53.
Translator.

*** Formerly called "tone", or "whole-tone". *Translator.*

† Formerly called "half-tone", or "semitone". *Translator.*

2

PHRYGIAN.

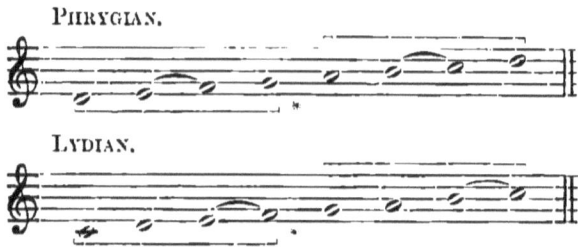

LYDIAN.

to which were subsequently added four more, respectively beginning on the remaining tones of the diatonic scale. In the above examples we find (at the *) a whole *step* between the two tetrachords: this was called *disjunctive* union. But a union may also be effected *conjunctively* — as the expression was — by making the highest tone of the lower tetrachord form at the same time the lowest one of the upper, and this procedure, applied to the Doric tetrachord, gave rise to a new system, viz: to the Doric octave-species were added a tetrachord below (*b c d e*) and one above (*e f g a*), and lastly, this series composed of two tetrachord-pairs was completed by adding the low *a* (called "Proslambanomenos", *i. e.,* the accessory tone), as in the following example:

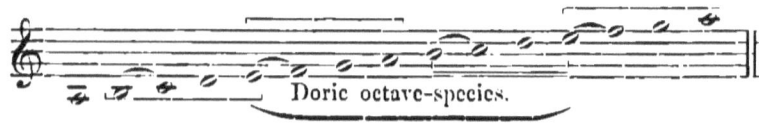
Doric octave-species.

Thus was gained a two-octave minor scale, a system substantially differing from the octave-species in that it can — like the modern major and minor scales — be transposed to each of the twelve tones (counting by half-steps) comprised within the Octave, the order of intervals remaining — unlike the case of the octave-species — always the same. This *transposing-scale* (Tonos) becomes the so-called *complete system* (systema teleion) by the addition of one more tetrachord (*a b♭ — c — d*), conjunctively with the parent tetrachord (*e f — g — a*), whereby the gap (the whole step *a — b*) at the meeting of both these tetrachords is filled up, and at the same time it is rendered possible to modulate into other keys (primarily into the Subdominant).

Complete System (Systema teleion).

The tone common to two tetrachords united *conjunctively* is called *Synaphe* (connecting-tone, or point of contact), the gap arising in the other case. *Diazeuxis* (Separation). Accordingly the tetrachord which is separated from its lower neighbor by a step is called *diezeugmenōn* (of the disjunct), and the interpolated one *synemmenōn* (of the conjunct, i. e. strings or tones).

We have thus indicated the chief points in which the Greek music-theory coincides with that of the Christian era; for, up to the time that two of the octave-species — the *Ionian* (our major scale and the *Æolian* (our minor scale) — attained the supremacy,* the octave-species collectively continued centuries long in use and have been retained in the Catholic liturgy even to the present time. Moreover we must emphasize as an essential difference between the antique and the modern music the incomparably greater *melodic variety* of the former. If the Greeks had no knowledge of harmony in the modern sense, i. e., polyphony, yet it seems as if, in compensation, their ear was from the melodic side very much more finely cultivated than ours. This is indicated by the various *tone-genera*,** which were formed within the Doric tetrachord by changing the place of the middle tone; thus from the *diatonic* genus *e f g a*, for instance, was formed the *chromatic*

---

* The need of reducing the seven octave-species to two specially characteristic ones was not fully satisfied until towards the end of the 17th century, yet it seems to have existed long before. This is indicated by the predominance of the two modes — major and minor — in the folk-songs of the most ancient tradition; moreover by a remark of PLATO, who, in his "Republic" (Book III, Chap. X, relates a conversation between SOCRATES and the musician GLAUKON concerning the character of the different octave-species, in the course of which SOCRATES, after characterizing two particular ones, concludes: "These two octave-species, a *powerful* one and a *gentle* one, which will best reproduce the tones of the unfortunate and the fortunate, of the thoughtful and the brave. let these be retained."

** The expression "tone-genus" has reference to the relative places, within the tetrachord, of the steps and the half-steps. (*Translator.*)

genus by lowering the *g*-string a half-step, and the *enharmonic**
by lowering *g* another half-step, and *f* a quarter-step, as here
exemplified, the × representing the quarter-step:

The richness, or more properly the polychromatic effect, of
the Greek melodies, was still farther increased by the application
of still smaller intervals, the so-called *Chroai* nuances', and
it is easily understood that the reigning spirit of the young Christian
church had to strive for a simplification of the musical system.
Not long after the afore-mentioned prohibition by CLEMENT OF AL-
EXANDRIA of the use of the chromatic genus, the Christian church
gives a second sign of musical life. The constant recurrence of
ecclesiastical holy-days had necessitated the adoption of certain
standards for the execution of church-song, and, in order to pre-
serve these for future generations also, the first-singing schools
were established by Pope SYLVESTER (A. D. 314) and his successor
HILARY. It was, moreover, all the more necessary to provide for
the education of church-singers, inasmuch as, owing to the adherence of the Church to the Latin language and the gradual
decay of the latter as vulgar tongue, the participation of the laity
in the church-song had of its own accord to cease, and in fact
soon afterward the council of Laodicea (A. D. 367) made a decree
that "no one should sing in church other than the singers appointed to do so from their pulpit".

Still more effectively than under those pontiffs was music fur-
thered in the same century under AMBROSE, Archbishop of Milan
(died A. D. 397), and two centuries later (590) under Pope GRE-
GORY THE GREAT. The former took an important step for the simplification of the music-system, by selecting for the use of divine
service, from among the Greek octave-species the four respectively

---

* Some authors, among them Fr. BELLERMANN, consider this genus an invention of bad singers, who had the mannerism of sliding from one tone to
another by passing through the intermediate intervals, — just as the *porta-
mento* is abused by bad singers of the present time.   *Translator.*

beginning with *d, e, f* and *g*, which were subsequently called *authentic modes*.* To these GREGORY added four more, respectively beginning with the Fourth below the authentic, which were called (from the Greek word "plagios", *i. e.* oblique, sidewise) *plagal* modes, collaterals, as it were, of the others.** Thus the number of the church-modes was increased to eight. It is to be observed, however, that the plagal are not independent keys in the same sense as the authentic; they are to be regarded as merely a transposition

---

* The expression "mode" corresponds to the modern "key", or "scale". It is applied also to a melody or chant, such as, for instance, is often called a Gregorian "tone". *Translator.*

** Here follow illustrations of these eight so-called "Ecclesiastical Modes", or "Gregorian Tones", the black notes representing the respective "finals" in the modern sense, key-notes. Changes of nomenclature will be noticed, the former Phrygian mode here becoming Dorian, and vice-versa, — etc. (compare Exs. p. 17). These changes are supposed to have been made about the 10th century. *Translator.*

of the former, in this wise, viz: that the lower part of the scale, containing the Fifth, remains in its place, while the upper part, containing the Fourth (Tetrachord), is transposed an Octave lower. The intimate connexion of an authentic with its plagal mode — a relationship admirably characterized by the writers of the Middle Age by means of the expressions "male" and "female" — is seen most clearly in the circumstance that the musical center of gravity, the "final", is common to both: the authentic mode has it in the lower part of its compass, the plagal, on the other hand, in the middle. The scale of the plagal modes, in other words, has its final (key-tone) on the *Fourth*, the melody roaming above and below it within the compass of an Octave. On this principle the melodies also were classified as "authentic" or "plagal", according as they extended from the final to its *Octave* and back, or, from the final to the *upper Fifth* and *lower Fourth*, ending, of course, on the final.*

Of the character of the *Ambrosian chant* we have no knowledge save through the meager accounts of contemporary writers, inasmuch as it was at an early date merged into the *Gregorian* and in time thoroughly amalgamated with it. From their descriptions we know only this much, that it was "solemn" and "extremely sweet", and for a while was more highly esteemed than even the chant of the Roman church; moreover it is called "metrical", by which is meant that it made account, after the ancient manner, of the prosodial quantity of the syllables, hereby essentially differing from the *Gregorian Chant*, in which the tones had no determinate length, and which was therefore also called *cantus planus*, *i. e.*, even or plain chant. True, this "evenness" of the Gregorian chant is not be taken too literally, as if no difference whatever was made in the duration of the notes; in fact, it was

---

* Accordingly, the respective first themes of SCHUBERT's E♭ Trio and BEETHOVEN's E♭ Symphony Eroica would belong to different modes, the former to the authentic, the latter to the plagal.

optional with the singer, especially as soloist, to treat the syllables of the text as in expressive speech, lengthening or shortening them at pleasure. Still, even here the restraints of prosody that hampered the antique music as also its near relation the *Ambrosian chant*, were thrown off. The liberation of music from the shackles of metrics, says DR. AMBROS (Geschichte der Musik, Vol. II), severed the tie that had up to that time bound the Christian music, to the antique, and the deep significance of ST. GREGORY'S musical reform lies in this, that music was now actually emancipated from poetry, in which it had hitherto made its appearance dependently, almost as integrant part.

The primacy that Pope GREGORY the GREAT had acquired for the Roman church brought about an ever greater spread of Christianity and simultaneously of the music connected with public worship. Both found an energetic protector in CHARLEMAGNE, that enlightened ruler who was able not only to subjugate nations resisting civilization, but also to elevate them intellectually. Rightly understanding that only the benefit of a higher culture could avail to reconcile permanently the conquered nations to his rule, he founded schools throughout the whole of his extensive kingdom, among which those at Metz, Soissons, Fulda, Mayence, Treves and St. Gall soon attained to high renown. At all these schools music was cultivated equally with the other branches of learning, principally as a science; but from the practical side also it was zealously fostered by the emperor, church-song as well as secular music. He caused his secretary EGINHARD to compile a collection of the heroic songs of his time, which unfortunately is lost; he had his daughter instructed in music three hours daily; he himself never failed to take part in the singing during public worship — in one of his portraits he appears in the midst of the choristers — and he repeatedly sent to Rome for chanters, that they might by their example refine the rough voices of his Frankish singers. Thus was the art of church-song enabled to develop itself more and more abundantly in the north of Europe also, especially in the school at Metz, which became greatly celebrated for its style of singing.

Of these art-missionaries sent from Rome there were two that laid the foundation for the musical splendor which the monastery of ST. GALL radiated during the period of intellectual darkness from the eighth to the twelfth century. PETRUS and ROMANUS were the names of the two singers who, by command of the Pope, and provided with an authentic transcript of the so-called *Antiphonary* — a collection of church-song prepared by ST. GREGORY — made a pilgrimage to the north for propagating the musical gospel. In crossing the Alps ROMANUS fell ill, and it was only with difficulty that he reached the monastery of ST. GALL: but here he was so affectionately cared for by the monks that even after his recovery he could not make up his mind to leave the hospitable abode, and — having obtained the Pope's permission — remained there to the end of his life, with him the Antiphonary, which to this day is preserved in the monastic library at ST. GALL. From this time forward begins among the monks of the monastery an unusually earnest scientific and artistic activity, the results of which are recorded by the chroniclers among them, most diffusely by EKKEHARD*, the fourth of this name. in his "Casus S. Galli", written about A. D. 1000. Much was done for the cultivation of music by the two NOTKERS especially, the one with the surname LABEO (the large-lipped), as author of the oldest treatise on music in the German (old High-German) language. the other, NOTKER BALBULUS (the stammerer , as inventor of a new art-species, the *Sequences*. The nature of this kind of melodies is indicated by their name: they were originally appendices, long-winded coloratures, with which the last tone of the "Hallelujah" was ornamented. These coloratures, which originally were improvised, grew in time to be regular melodies, to which. for better memorizing them, words were adapted. One of these melodies arranged and supplied with text by NOTKER BALBULUS, has not only been retained in the Catholic church-service but also passed over into the Protestant (Lutheran) choral-song: it is the sequence "Media vita in morte sumus" (in German. "Mitten wir im Leben sind von dem Tod umfangen": in English, "In the midst of life we are by death surrounded"), to the writing of which NOTKER received the impulse when on a ramble in the wild chasm near ST. GALL. the so-called "Martinstobel" (Martin's

---

* VICTOR SCHEFFEL has utilised the accounts given by this historian for a vivid description of the monastic life at St. Gall in his romance entitled "Ekkehard".

glen), at the sight of a workman who was killed there while building a bridge.

Besides vocal music, instrumental performance also was industriously practised in the monastery of ST. GALL. Of the monk TUOTILO the chronicle relates that he played quite skilfully on various kinds of wind and stringed instruments, and instructed the young nobles of the neighborhood in the use of them. Here, as in the North generally, instrumental music was sure to find many lovers for the reason that the climate was less favorable than that of the countries of southern Europe to the development of the vocal organs, and consequently the sweetness of the Italian singing was denied to the northern voices. That in this respect the singers of ST. GALL also, for all the ripeness of their musical culture, had to stand in the background, is shown by the words of a traveller from Italy who, after an evening musical performance during his stay in the monastery, wrote in his diary: "The men this side of the Alps, though they make the thunder of their voices to roar towards heaven, can never mount to the sweetness of soft modulation. Truly barbarous is the roughness of these throats, hardened by drink; when they try, by lowering and raising the tone, to sing with sweetness, nature shudders, and it sounds like a wagon rattling over the frozen pavement in wintertime".

The author of this sharp criticism hardly dreamed, perhaps, that the northerners so despised by him had a mission to enrich music with one of its most important accessories. It was in the north of Europe that that element was to be developed which may be regarded as precisely the characteristic feature of the modern as distinguished from the ancient music, viz: *polyphony*. The following section will show how insignificant were the germs from which — only, it is true, after the lapse of many centuries of hard labor — the art could shoot forth whose climax is indicated by the name of PALESTRINA.

III.
THE BEGINNINGS OF POLYPHONIC MUSIC.

Before we more closely consider the advances made in music by the northern nations, we must make mention of another people, which during the centuries of mediæval storm and stress exercised a fostering influence — if not specially upon music, at least — upon the development of culture in general, viz: the *Arabians*. The capacity of this race to participate in the intellectual labor of humanity is indicated even by the writers of antiquity. But these qualifications attained their full development only in consequence of the religious and social reform brought about by MAHOMET (A. D. 622); under its influence the Orient was able to lift itself within a short time to a plane of civilization to which Europe was to attain only after centuries later. Nor did it suffice to the followers of Islam to establish only on their native soil sites which, like Bagdad and Damascus, spread over the world the fame of oriental culture and civilization; in the very next century they were impelled to propagate the doctrine of the prophet even beyond their own part of the globe. In a trice North-Africa as far as the Pillars of Hercules was subjugated, and after crossing the Straits of Gibraltar (A. D. 711) an end was put to the Gothic rule in Spain, which had already been strongly shaken by party quarrels. The kingdom of the Caliphs arose from the ruins and attained with surprising rapidity to a high political and intellectual prominence, and its capital city Cordova was soon able to take rank with the previously mentioned centres of culture of the Orient. The Arabians distinguished themselves pre-eminently by fostering the sciences, in which the numerous Jews residing in Spain could aid them all the more effectually on account of not being, for their part, impeded in their intellectual activity by any kind of material pressure, as they were later, in consequence of religious fanaticism under the Christian rulers of the land.

For the rest of Europe the sovereignty of Islam in Spain came to be of great importance through the circumstance, above everything else, that by the agency of the scholars residing in Spain the rest of Europe became acquainted — primarily, to be sure, in Latin versions only — with the literature of Grecian antiquity. The artistic influence also of the Spanish Arabians on the neighboring peoples cannot have been insignificant, to judge by their performances in the domain of architecture, whose importance and unique character are attested by the monuments which are still extant, especially the grand mosque at Cordova and the royal palace of the Alhambra at Granada. From doing as much for *music* the Arabians appear to have been hindered by that medley of soberness and grotesqueness which characterizes oriental art in general. The same spirit of restriction that is seen in the ornamentation of their edifices, and which, for keeping inviolate the law of the Koran against symbolical representations of natural objects, changes every ornament into mathematical figures — called, after their inventors, arabesques — this spirit is expressed in the oriental music also with its exuberance of ornamentation, and hinders it from attaining to solid structures. Just as little, however, as the practical music of the Arabs, was their musical theory (although, as Dr. AMBROS says, not a whit behind that of the ancient Greeks in subtlety and intricacy) able to afford any starting-point whatever for a musical reorganization.

To labor creatively in this sense was reserved to the *Nations of the North*. If nature had denied them the euphony of the southern voices, they had received, in compensation, the talent for tone-combinations of every kind, in a higher degree than the inhabitants of southern Europe. Let us here once more refer to the significance of *instrumental music* in relation to that talent. In the first place the instruments afforded, with their fixed number of strings, or — in the case of wind-instruments — holes, a much surer foot-hold to theoretical speculation than the human voice, which can wander through intervals of infinitely different extent: but the influence of instrumental performance upon musical composition was in a high degree stimulating and purifying, first, because the instruments allow to the composer's imagination freer play than the vocal setting, cramped by the limited compass of the human voice as also by the text; then too because a piece of music without words has quite special need of inner coherence, so as not to degenerate into empty trifling. We may accordingly assume without hesitation that polyphonic music took its starting-point not from the land of song but from that of instrumental music, and that it was practically executed on instruments long before any one began to apply it in song or to treat it theoretically.

The correctness of the latter assumption is vouched for moreover by the nature of the bow-instruments as they appear on the oldest monuments. The viols here represented have mostly three strings; but as the bridge is flat and the depressions introduced in the modern violin-body are lacking, the bow necessarily had to touch all three strings at once, thus producing a tone-combination like that which is still heard on the Scotch bag-pipe and the hurdy-gurdy of our time: on the highest string a melody was played, while the two lower ones sustained the key-tone and its Fifth, after the manner of an "organ-point". That the first attempts in polyphonic singing, originally improvisations of a second voice to a melody of the Gregorian church-song, were instigated by the playing of such instruments is indicated by the name applied to them — "*ars organandi*" (literally, art of "organating"*), for in early mediæval times by "Organum" was meant any species of musical instrument. And for the same reason the word "organum" was applied to the art of polyphonic composition, at the time that it found in the Flemish monk HUCBALD, or UBALDUS (died A. D. 930 in St. Amand's monastery, Flanders) its first theoretical representative.

HUCBALD's doctrine of the *Organum*, or — as he also calls it — *Diaphony*, treats of polyphonic music, and that not only as the mere singing in Octaves or the occasional concent of a second tone, as had been practised by the Greeks, but as the simultaneous sounding of different tone-series, — in a word, as that

---

* A barbarous English word coined from a barbarous Latin original. The expression "organising", in common use, seems to me hardly appropriate here.
 Translator.

which at the present day we mean by the word "Harmony".* The interval best adapted to such progressions was found by HUCBALD to be the Fifth, already acknowledged by the ancients as a consonance, and accordingly he began by making two voices move in parallel Fourths or Fifths. Next, by doubling the lower voice in the upper Octave he obtained a three-voiced setting and parallel Fourths, and Fifths, and finally, by doubling the Fourths or Fifths, a four-voiced setting.**

---

* In antiquity by "Harmony" was understood every regular tone-series; even toward the close of the Middle Age the Netherlandic music-theorist TINCTORIS defines harmony as "the same as melody". — Of HUCBALD's Organum it has been maintained of late that it is not to be regarded as harmony in the modern sense of the word; that its tone-series moving in parallel Fifths were not meant to be simultaneous but successive. The alleged proofs of this assertion are, first, the offensiveness, to the musically cultivated ear, of parallel Fifths; and secondly, the Latin predicates "praecedens" and "subsequens" respectively applied to the two tone-series by the writers of that time. To the first point, it is answered that musical taste changes; hence what is offensive to modern ears may have been agreeable to those who lived a thousand years ago. As to the Latin words it is to be observed that they may mean not only "preceding" and "subsequent", but also "principal" and "imitating". In the present case they have undoubtedly the latter meaning, for HUCBALD's mission, and that of the Middle Age in general was — not to revive the ancient antiphonal or responsive singing, but to establish a theoretical foundation for an entirely different kind of music, viz: for the simultaneous combination of the intervals and for the connexion of these tone-combinations.

** Examples of this curious system, as illustrations of the beginnings of harmony, are lacking in the original; I have therefore given the following ones.
Translator.

If we have here merely a purely mechanical tone-combination, another kind of Organum, called "oblique",[*] exhibits an approach to artistic form. This latter kind is invariably only two-voiced, and consists partly of parallel Fourths, partly of oblique motion, the lower voice, that is, remaining on one tone while the upper one forms with it a Second, Third, Unison, etc.[**] True, even this did not contribute much to the advancement of the new art, although HUCBALD himself had no doubt as to the glorious effect of his Organum. "If two or more of you" — he says — "shall sing together with discreet and harmonious strictness, each

Mi - se - re - re   me - i, De - us.

Four-voiced.

in o - pe - ri - bus su - is.   Tu Patris sempiternus es Fi-li-us.

[*] In contradistinction, that is, to the first kind, in which, as the examples show, the voices move invariably in strict parallelism.   *Translator.*

[**] In this system parallel *Thirds* were strictly forbidden, which need not seem so very strange to us when we consider that according to the system of tuning of that time every major Third was too sharp and every minor Third too flat. Hence the Third was regarded as a *dissonant* interval. As the original of this work gives no example of this kind of harmonization, this defect is hereby made good.   *Translator.*

Two-voiced.

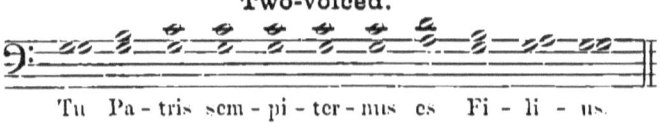

Tu Pa - tris sem - pi - ter - nus   es   Fi - li - us.

Four-voiced.

Tu Pa - tris sem - pi - ter - nus   es   Fi - li - us.

carrying his own part, you will notice a delightful concent arising from this blending of tones." — With similar meagre results (as we of our day should put it) HUCBALD had to be satisfied in his attempt to improve *musical notation*. The marking of the tones by means of the first seven letters of the alphabet, which was usual in his time, having been introduced by GREGORY the GREAT, could no longer suffice for the higher aims which music henceforth pursued, any more than could the so-called *Neumes*, a kind of notation which probably arose from the accents of the Greek written language. This notation, consisting of countless characters, dots, little strokes and hooks, had, to be sure, this advantage over the letter-signs that it could represent the height and depth of the tones, yet the position of the several tone-signs was, in the absence of a system of lines (staff), so indefinite as to allow the most diverse readings. HUCBALD's first attempt at reform in this sphere, scarcely more than a modification of the Greek letter-notation, necessarily failed of success for the very reason that here no provision was made for the need just alluded to, the symbolization of the rise and fall of the tones. This service was rendered, it is true, by a system of notation afterwards proposed by him, having a *staff* on which the text-syllables were piled up and the tone-degrees indicated by the letters **T** *Tonus*, whole step and **S** *Semitonium*, half-step! at the beginning of each space; yet this system was just as little able to supplant the neume-notation, especially on account of its clumsiness, as exhibited in the following example,*

Tono			
T	Ǎ	Al \	
Tono	F̌	le \	u \
Tono	I	lu |	i \
Sono	F̌		a \
Tono	F̌		a

translated as follows into modern notation:

Al - le - lu - i - a.

* The signs found after the letters **T** and **S** belong to HUCBALD's above-mentioned first attempt at reform in music-notation, and are fully explained by H. BELLERMANN, in the *Allgemeine musikalische Zeitung* (Leipsic, 1868, No. 37.

It was not till a century later that the need of an intelligible music-notation was supplied, through the agency of Guido d'Arezzo, who was the first one to use a staff of four lines, employing not only these but also the spaces, and thus gaining for each tone of the diatonic scale its own fixed place. He carried out to a conclusion the attempts of his predecessors, who in utilizing the lines had not followed any fixed principle, and thus he became the creator of the system of notation still in use at the present time: for now ensued a simplification of both the number and the form of the neume-signs, which finally after all sorts of modifications were transformed into the modern notes, as, for example, the *virgula* (a figure resembling a comma) into our modern quarter-note. — Still greater, at least, among his contemporaries, was the reputation acquired by Guido on account of his method of teaching singing, by means of which, as was asserted, the pupil could learn in three days as much as previously would have required as many weeks. This method consisted in drilling the learner in an unknown melody by comparison with another one already known to him. As such a typical melody Guido recommended a certain hymn whose separate melodic phrases — or, in modern language, "measures" — form, in their initial tones, a diatonic scale. The text-syllables respectively corresponding to these initial tones are: *ut, re, mi, fa, sol, la,** which casual circumstance gave occasion to the Romance nations to name the diatonic scale after these syllables (the *si,* for the seventh degree, was added later in France, after the octave-system had been generally accepted). The advantage which precisely this hymn offered

---

* This hymn, in which the singers beg St. John the Baptist to deliver them from hoarseness, runs thus:

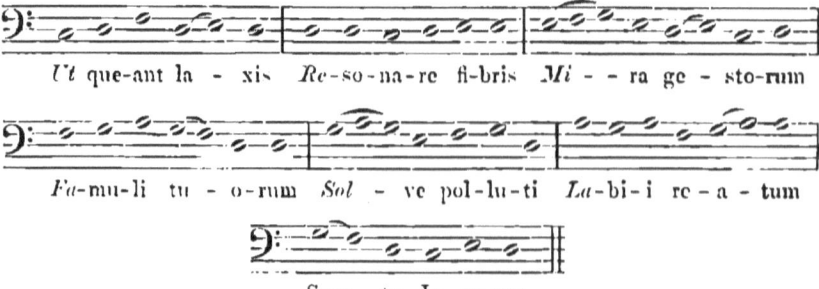

the pupil was a twofold one, as it not only afforded him opportunity to memorize the scale, but was also calculated to quicken the ear for the difference between the church-modes, for which latter, as for the melodic phrases of the hymn, the varying position of the intervals forms the characteristic feature.

The success of this method was so great that even the Pope (John XIX. 1024—1033) wished to learn it, and invited its discoverer to Rome by three messengers, received him on his arrival in the most friendly manner and did not rise from his seat till he had correctly learned a melody previously unknown to him, and thus experienced personally what he had hardly been willing to believe on the word of others — as GUIDO narrates in a letter to his friend and fellow-monk Michael. A great part of GUIDO's success must, however, be set down to the score of his personality; for although he belonged, like all other representatives of art and science in the Middle Age, to the clerical state — at first in the monastery of Pomposa near Ravenna, afterwards in that of the Benedictines at Arezzo — yet he by no means restricted himself in his labors to the cloister-cell, but exerted himself unremittingly in order that his musical achievements might accrue to the advantage of the whole world. He is mainly distinguished from all his contemporaries in that he was a man of the people, and as such he was praised by the grateful voice of the masses for centuries after his death, and even far above his desert. In fact, a whole series of inventions belonging to later times are ascribed to him by the musicographers even of the preceding century, among other things the so-called *harmonic* or *Guidonian hand*, which appears from the 12th century onward in all musical instruction-books. The object of this invention was to enable the student to learn the names of the tones employed in GUIDO's time, each one of these, except *B flat* and *ee*, being assigned to a place on one of the nineteen joints of the human hand (the finger-tips being included): the upper joint of the thumb took Gamma (Γ), then downward (*A*, *B*), then across (*C*, *D*, *E*, *F*), up the little finger (*G*, *a*, *b*), along the upper joints of the next three fingers (*c*, *d*, *e*), down the little finger again (*f*, *g*), and so on, in a circle, up to the highest tone but one: the last, *ee*, had its place above the middle finger.

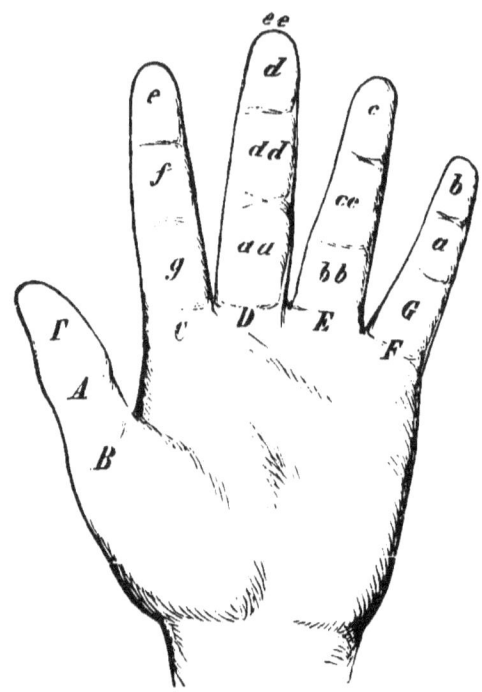

Of incomparably greater value is another invention ascribed to Guido, the system of *Solmisation* (*Sol-faing*), which deserves to be mentioned here for the special reason that it was held in high esteem by practical as well as theoretical musicians long after the Middle Age. The Solmisation or *Hexachord-system* divides the tone-series (extended soon after Guido to 20 tones) into seven groups of six degrees each, called Hexachords, the several tones of which are called *ut, re, mi, fa, sol, la*. These Hexachords are, however, not joined together as the Octaves are in our modern system (for this would give a series of 42 tones), but *overlap* each other; the lowest (the so-called *Hard* Hexachord) embraces the tones Γ (Gamma,* or G, the tone added below the scale originally beginning with A), A, B, C, D, E; but already on the fourth degree, C, begins a new one, the *Natural* Hexachord, viz: C, D, E, F, G, a, and on the fourth degree, F, of this Hexachord a third, the *Soft* Hexachord. The last designation

---

* This tone being called *gamma-ut*, originated our English word *gamut*.
                                                                Translator.

has no reference to the interval-succession, which is here the same as in the two other Hexachords, but to the "soft B" (our B flat, called B molle), a tone inserted in the scale to make the half-step occur, as usual, between its third and fourth tones, and thus to avoid the so-called *Tritone*, or major Fourth, $f - b$. On the next degree, G, is then repeated the "Hard" Hexachord, then the "Natural" and the "Soft", closing with the seventh Hexachord, which as being the highest is called *super-acutum*, whilst the Hexachords of the lowest Octaves are called *grave*, those next above them *acutum*. All this is illustrated in the following figure.*

Hex. 1, hard, grave.	Hex. 2, natural, grave.	Hex. 3, soft, grave.	Hex. 4, hard, acute.	Hex. 5, natural, acute.	Hex. 6, soft, acute.	Hex. 7, hard, super-acute.	The Gamut.
					e la		e la.
				d la	d sol		d la sol.
				c sol	c fa		c sol fa.
				b♭ fa	b♮ mi		b fa. b mi.
			a la	a mi	a re		a la mi re.
			g sol	g re	g ut		g sol re ut.
			f fa	f ut			f fa ut.
		e la	e mi				e la mi.
	d la	d sol	d re				d la sol re.
	c sol	c fa	c ut				c sol fa ut.
	b♭ fa	b♮ mi					b fa. b mi.
a la	a mi	a re					a la mi re.
G sol	G re	G ut					G sol re ut.
F fa	F ut						F fa ut.
E la	E mi						E la mi.
D sol	D re						D sol re
C fa	C ut						C fa ut.
B mi							B mi.
A re							A re.
Γ ut							Γ ut.

* I have given the illustration in the form found in GROVE'S "Dictionary

The attachment to the tetrachord-system of the Greeks seems to have been one reason why the octave-system was not already adopted and a kind of transition by means of the hexachord was preferred. Nevertheless the sol-faing, in that it lays stress on the intimate relations between the principal key and its collateral keys (Tonic, Dominant and Subdominant), was by no means unimportant for the evolution of the modern music-system, and it is no wonder that even at the beginning of the last century it found ardent defenders, among them the excellent organist BUTTSTEDT, of Erfurt.

Despite the improvements in music-notation introduced by GUIDO OF AREZZO, one imperfection still adhered to it which with the advancing cultivation of polyphonic music was necessarily more and more keenly felt — the impossibility of indicating the *duration of the tones*. If two or more parts were to be sung together, their relative proportion had to be accurately determined, in regard not only to the pitch of the tones but also to their time-value. The first writer to give information regarding the rules to be observed in "mensural" music is FRANCO OF COLOGNE (about A. D. 1200). Like all his predecessors in the province of music-theory he too follows the Greek tradition and admits at first only two note-values, the long and the short note (*longa* ■ and *brevis* ■), corresponding to the long and the short syllable of the ancient prosody. The union of these two notes, the shorter of which has half the value of the longer, gives the so-called *modus*, which appears either as trochee (— ◡) or as iambus (◡ —), and is always tripartite. This explains why in the earliest period of mensural music the three-part rhythm alone found application, and, after the two-part rhythm also came into use later on, was called "perfect", the latter "imperfect". In carrying out his system farther, however, FRANCO forsakes the ancient traditions, for here appear as new note-values the *double long* (maxima ■■) and the *half short semibrevis* ♦). With these signs, to which are to be added those for the *rests*, which also are mentioned for the first time by FRANCO, it was now possible to note down a rhythmically variegated piece of music. The mensural notation labored, however, under the imperfection that the value of the notes depended not only on their

---

of Music and Musicians" Art. "Hexachord" as being clearer than that in the original. *Translator.*

shape but also on their *position in regard to the neighboring note.* Thus, a *long* alone filled a tripartite measure: but if followed by a *short*, or *breve* it became bipartite and together with the latter formed a measure; if followed by two breves it again became tripartite, the two breves then forming together a tripartite measure, in this way, that the first one had the value of one part, the second one, of two parts.*

After FRANCO OF COLOGNE the greatest services in the development of mensural music were rendered by MARCHETTUS OF PADUA (end of the 13th century) and JOHANNES DE MURIS, doctor of theology at the Paris university (beginning of the 14th century). In the writings of these two learned musicians appears for the first time the prohibition of the parallel Octaves and Fifths so praised by HUCBALD for their sweetness, together with other rules which have remained to this day in force for strict composition. DE MURIS is said also to have first applied the word *counterpoint* (*i. e.*, "point against point",** in Latin "punctus contra punctum") instead of the word "discant", in use up to that time, to denote a two-voiced composition. The one-sided preference for the tripartite measure is, to be sure, manifested by him: it is not till a century later that the bipartite measure is introduced in practical composition as of equal right with the former, and thus the required free space was gained for the farther development of mensural music.

Let this little suffice to give an idea of the helplessness of the mensural notation and the laboriousness of the intellectual work of the Middle Age in general, even at the time of the meritorious personages already mentioned. We are just in the palmy days of the *scholastic philosophy*, which from the time of

---

* A rhythm of this kind ■ ■ ■ ▪ ■ ■, expressed in modern notation seems, to be sure, to modern ears not a little strange on account of the clumsy limping movement; but taken in quick time it loses this character, as is seen in many examples of its application in modern compositions, as for instance in the first movement of BEETHOVEN's Symphony in *A* (No. 7).

** This refers to the ancient manner of notation by pricking the paper, thus forming points, which represented notes. *Translator.*

CHARLEMAGNE to the revival of the ancient culture, thus six hundred years long, ruled the world. During this period, in which the church, grown more and more powerful, had rendered both science and art tributary to herself alone, philosophical thought and dialectics are also found exclusively in the service of theology: philosophy is regarded as the serving-maid (ancilla) of religion, and even the study of the ancient authors, especially of ARISTOTLE, had for its sole purpose the scientific support of the edifice of Christian faith erected by the fathers of the church. No wonder that under an intellectual tendency so unfavorable to the investigation of truth, humanity, in its endeavors after progress, should often go astray, and the inquirer not seldom lose himself in petty speculation and trifles. Thus a HUCBALD could hit upon the whimsical idea of composing in honor of CHARLES THE BALD a Latin poem, "The praise of baldness", in which every word had the same initial letter — c — as the Latin word for baldness — *calvities*; thus too could the practical GUIDO recommend a method of composition which consisted in substituting for each of the five vowels a tone of the scale, and then writing under the several syllables of a text chosen at option the tone corresponding to its vowel, whereby, according to his opinion, every thing written was changed into song — a "manikin-melodization in the retort of the five vowels", as Dr. AMBROS has very happily characterized this manner of composing. FRANCO, too, is seen to be by no means free from the scholastic usage of referring every thing to the church; as when for instance he maintains that the tripartite *longa* ■) is to be called the "perfect" because it took its name from the Holy Trinity, the absolute and true perfection. But MARCHETTO OF PADUA even drags the christian doctrine into the dispute whether the tripartite long note should have the stem on the right or the left side, and settles the matter in favor of the right side thus: "As the right side in man is more perfect than the left, because it contains that which nourishes and perfects man, to wit, the blood; so too a note with the stem at the right side is more perfect than one with the stem at the left. For this reason too, Christ willed to be pierced in the right side, in order to shed all his blood for the human race".

Still, for all the unfavorable conditions of the time, the stagnation of the intellectual life was in appearance only: slowly, but surely, the world moved forward to higher aims. Scholasticism, too, had to contribute its share to the movement of minds, in that it made the objects of faith objects first of reason, then of doubt, lastly of scientific investigation. Indeed, the very vagaries of the scholastics tell of thirst for light and the spirit of inquiry, which under the pressure of circumstances could of course reveal themselves for the most part only in the petty manner just alluded to. But, just as science in consequence of these endeavors struggled up to new life, so did also art, particularly music, for which, after the accomplishment of the needful preliminary labors, that epoch of rich development began which is called, after the nation chiefly concerned in it, the **Netherlandic**.

IV.
THE MUSICAL SOVEREIGNTY OF THE NETHERLANDERS.

Through the labors of a HUCBALD, a GUIDO and a FRANCO the soil in which a genuine art-music could grow up was, indeed, prepared, yet it was a considerable time before the first buds of such a thing ventured to show themselves. The European nations were still too deeply sunken in lethargy and barbarity to allow to art free space for its development: when all at once an event happened which powerfully transformed not only the religious and political situation, but also the collective intellectual life of Europe, that is to say, the *Crusades*, beginning in 1096. It was not only to the members of the religious and the knightly orders that the summons of a PETER OF AMIENS, a BERNARD OF CLAIRVAUX for the rescue of the holy sepulchre from the hands of the infidels was addressed: to all who should join the expedition eternal salvation was promised, and in consequence of this, multitudes belonging to the most diverse conditions of life who were eager for the adventure took part in the march to Jerusalem, as in a general pilgrimage. For the great majority of the Crusaders, however, the impressions and experiences gained in the East must have had a lasting effect, since, as has already been mentioned, the civilization of that country was, even from the reign of the Abassides, especially of the caliph HAROUN AL RASCHID (A. D. 800), who belonged to that dynasty, in every respect superior to that of the West. Similarly, the singers and instrumental musicians in the retinue of the Crusaders found in the East rich inspiration and nutriment for their art. For, although the oriental music — like that of the Arabs in Spain — was of its very nature ill-adapted to the solution of ideal art-problems, yet the singing-method of the orientals with its characteristic richness of ornamentation, as also their musical instruments the lute and the guitar, which had been unknown to the Crusaders, moreover the noisy instruments used in the Saracen military music, the drum and the kettle-drum. — all these elements, after they had been introduced into the western music, necessarily gave the latter an altered character.

Still more important appears to be the enrichment experienced by the *poetry* of the West in consequence of the Crusades. The separation — often for years — from home and family brought about a deepening of the emotional life till then unknown: a new species of poetry arises in which the feeling for chivalry and love-service (Minnedienst) finds its expression, the so-called *gay science* (*gaya ciencia*, indigenous especially to the soil of Provence, favored as it is by a happy climate and the lively disposition of its inhabitants.* Here the grandees of the land devoted themselves to this science, the first being count WILLIAM OF POITIERS (1087—1127), afterwards king THIBAUT OF NAVARRE (1201—1254), these, however, always only as *originators* of songs, whence they were also called *Trouvères* (from the French "trouver", a word which has become in our English tongue (more identical with the Italian synonym "trovatore") *Troubadours*. The *execution* of the songs composed by them, as also the instrumental accompaniment of them they handed over to the so-called *Minstrels* (derived from "ministerialis", from the Latin "minister", a "helper"), also called *Jongleurs* (from the Latin "joculator", merry-maker), who belonged to a lower class of society and were often ranked with buffoons, as is seen in a contemporaneous sculpture of the church of St. George at Bocherville near Rouen, representing among a group of instrumental musicians a human figure walking on his hands. An exceptional position among the troubadours is occupied by ADAM DE LA HALE, called after his deformity and his native place "the humpback of Arras", inasmuch as he unites in his person the

---

* The cradle of this art may probably be held to be the court of the margraves of Barcelona, whose kingdom, founded by CHARLEMAGNE as a rampart against the Arab dominion in Spain, stood in intimate political and intellectual relations with southern France, especially with Provence, but was at the same time directly exposed to the influence of Arabic civilization, which also on its part had an important share in the development of Provencial song.

composer of songs and the executive musician. He was moreover well versed in the strict art-forms also, so far as they had then been developed, and ranks among the first musicians who undertook to compose four-voiced vocal pieces. A lately discovered vaudeville by him, "Robin and Marian", the subject of which is the naive description of a rustic love-affair, was performed in 1282 at the court of Robert the second of Artois at Naples, and is therefore the oldest specimen of dramatic art in France, for which reason ADAM DE LA HALE is rightfully indicated in the history of French literature as the founder of comic opera.

The same intellectual current that in the case of the Romanic peoples had called into existence the art of the troubadours, expressed itself among the ancient Germans who had remained unmixed in Germany, in the form of erotic poetry called in their tongue *Minnegesang*.*) The "minnesinger" differed, however, from the troubadour in that he himself sang his songs and accompanied them on an instrument, usually a small three-cornered harp, such as is often seen depicted in ancient manuscripts, among others in that of GODFREY OF STRASBURG'S "Tristan and Isolt", belonging to the first half of the 13th century, in the court-library at Munich. Moreover the minnesingers did not belong, as the troubadours did, exclusively to the knightly order; of the singers participating in the *Sängerkrieg auf der Wartburg* (contest of singers on the Wartburg), in 1207, under landgrave Hermann of Thuringia, WOLFRAM OF ESCHENBACH, WALTER OF THE VOGELWEIDE, HEINRICH SCHREIBER and HEINRICH OF ZWETZSCHIN were, as the chronicler puts it, "knightly men", on the other hand BITEROLF was one "of the landgrave's household servants", and HEINRICH OF OFTERDINGEN a burgess of Eisenach. The musical difference of the German Minnegesang or love-song from the song of the troubadour consisted in this, that the latter made the text subservient to the melody, whereas with the former the poetry becomes the principal thing and the characteristic song-melody is supplanted by the recitative style of the ecclesiastical chant.

This predominance of the poetical over the musical element is exhibited also in the songs of the *Master-singers*, who under-

---

*) From "Minne", love, and "Gesang", song. It is generally englished "Minnesong".   *Translator.*

took the care of art after it had passed over from the knightly singers to the burghers and respectable artisans. According to F. H. von der Hagen ("The Minne-singers and Song-poets of the 13th, 14th and 15th centuries". Leipsic, 1838. Vol. IV, p. 853 seqq.). by the so-called "tones" of the master-singers are meant not only the song-melodies themselves, but also the metrical schemes, hence they have special reference to the poetry. Concerning the interior economy of these singing-societies organised after the manner of a guild, we find copious information in Wagenseil's book "Von der Meistersinger holdseligen Kunst" ("Of the delightful art of the Master-singers") published 1697 in Nuremberg, and in our own time Richard Wagner has renewed the memory of the Master-singers in his poem bearing that title. In these works we are made acquainted in the first place with the *Tabulature*, by which is meant the whole body of laws for the government of the guild. The members are divided into three classes: whoever has learned the various "tones" is a "singer"; a higher degree, the rank of a "poet", is attained by him who composes a new and suitable text to one of the tones; but to acquire the dignity of "master" the union of both faculties, the poetical and the musical, is requisite:

> "The poet who, with brain so witty,
> To words and rhymes. by himself prepared,
> Can shape from the tones a new strain or ditty,
> He is a "Master-singer" declared."*

The conscientiousness and the zeal shown by the members of the guild in the observance of their laws can serve as a gratifying testimony to the feeling for art entertained by the German burgherdom, even though the artistic results of those efforts have only extremely little value. The melodies of the Master-singers were like the church psalmody, monotonous and lacking in expression, although they were embellished at the cadencing sections with all kinds of ornamentation. The relation of their music to poetry was as good as none at all; as a rule the tune was not determined by the text, but vice-versa, the text by the tune: frequently

---

* From Wagner's "Die Meistersinger von Nürnberg", englished by H. and F. Corder. I take this opportunity of saying that the brothers Corder have in my judgment admirably succeeded in the difficult task of reproducing in English the wit and raciness of Wagner's original.   *Translator.*

the tune was composed first, and after it was found to be free of faults the author was required to make a suitable text to it, upon a determined biblical or spiritual subject. With this homely manner of art-education, which moreover is manifested in the strange names given to the tunes — there was, for instance, "an Over-short evening-red tune", a "Black ink tune", a "Short monkey tune", a "Gormandizer-in-secret tune", etc. — neither poetry nor music could specially thrive. Yet the master-singer schools had unquestionably a good effect on the morality of their members, and much as we may feel repelled by the pedantry inherent in their artistic efforts, yet on the other hand the tendency of these simple natures, aiming at the ideal in the midst of all the worry of common-place life, deserves the warmest recognition. This view is taken by RICHARD WAGNER also when he makes his master-singer HANS SACHS (1495—1576) answer as follows the question as to the rules of the Guild): "By what man were they first devised?"

> "By certain sorely troubled masters,
> Their hearts oppressed by life's disasters;
> By suffering overweighted,
> A model they created.
> That they might take it,
> And ever make it
> A memory of youthful love,
> In which the soul of Spring should move." *

The schools of the Master-singers fell, after the Thirty Years' War, more and more into decay; only those of Nuremberg and Strasburg maintained, up to the close of the preceding century, a certain importance. The German master-song did not actually come to an end before 1839, when the last surviving members of the School at Ulm handed over their corporation badges to the Liederkranz of that city and thereby dissolved their guild. The master-singers were moreover of advantage to the music of their time in this respect, that, after their example the instrumental musicians also united in corporations organized like guilds, gave up the wandering life which they had previously led and took up a permanent abode in the cities. Thus arose, as early as 1288, in Vienna a society under the name of the "*Nicolai-Bruderschaft*",

---

* "Die Meistersinger von Nürnberg". Corder's translation.

and in 1330 in Paris the "*Confrérie de St. Julien des Ménestriers*" (Minstrels), the latter under a director with the title of "King of the violins" (roi des violons), whose rule continued till the 17th century, when it was terminated by LOUIS XIV, after the last director, DUMANOIR II., had arrogated the jurisdiction over all the musicians of Paris, including the organists, and thus brought on himself his downfall.

Side by side with the Minnesong and the Master-song, but independent of either, the *Folksong* (National Song) had in the last centuries of the Middle Age been developed. The so-called Limburg Chronicle, edited by the scribe JOHANNES (1317—1402), gives the earliest details concerning the nature of the Folksongs and of the contemporaneous instrumental music ("pipe-playing", as it calls it), but unfortunately no musical specimens: these, however, are found in great number in a manuscript of the 15th century, called, after the place where it originated, the "Lochheim song-book". The melodies therein given are remarkable not only for the significant tone-leading and the skilfully organized rhythms, but also for the fidelity with which they reproduce the subject-matter of the poetry and give expression to that which language is unable of itself alone to utter.

If now we return to the consideration of *Art-music*, we again see an ecclesiastico-historical event coincide with the evolutionary course of music — the emigration, necessitated by the political dismemberment of Italy, of the papal see from Rome to Avignon (1305). Here, in music-loving Provence, the need of utilizing for the service of the Church also the musical advances made in the course of the ages could not but find rich nourishment. In particular, the till then only timidly practised art of "Organating" (see p. 28) is now, under the name of *Discantus* (song of two, *i. e.*, two-voiced song), studied by the church-singers with more and more freedom and zeal, so that not unfrequently the dignity of the divine service seemed to be compromised by it. In vain did Pope JOHN XXII issue a bull against the use of strange and unmelodic intervals in the Gregorian chant, "with the exception of certain more melodious consonances, such as the Octave, Fifth and Fourth, applied to the simple church-song, and even these on festivals only". It was not until the middle of the fourteenth century that the rules for the discant, which had already been laid down a century before, were fully recognised in practice also, owing chiefly to the efforts of Frenchmen and Netherlanders in the papal chapel who were specially endowed for this art, and herewith the abuse of improvising was for the time being kept within bounds. In this period originates the oldest example of tetraphonic, or four-voiced church-music, a mass composed for the coronation of Charles V. of France (1364) by WILLIAM OF MACHAUD, who, as previously ADAM DE LA HALE, constitutes the transition from the troubadour to the really schooled musician. Of the several voices of such a tetraphonic vocal piece, that one which sustained the principal melody, or *Cantus firmus*, taken from the Gregorian chant, was called *Tenor* (from the Latin "tenere", "to hold". As this principal melody was assigned by preference to the clearer species of male voice, the name "Tenor" has adhered to this species although its original signification necessarily disappeared with the later development of polyphonic music. The counter-part, the *Discantus* or *Cantus*, was also called *Motetus*, from the French "mot", i. e., sentence, or motto, inasmuch as it was usual to employ for this voice a motive borrowed from some popular song, the text of which bore some relation to that of the church-melody. The third, highest voice was called *Triplum* whence the English expression "Treble" for the soprano part of a tetraphonic vocal piece), and the fourth additional voice, *Quadruplum*. The two latter voices are, however, occasionally called, respectively, *Superius* and *Contra-tenor*.

A form of three-voiced song had already, under the name of *Faux-Bourdon* (in English "Faburden", found favor with the papal singers: it is thus described by the Milanese theorist FRANCHINUS GAFOR died 1522: "When the Tenor and the Cantus move in one or more Sixths: the middle voice, to wit, the Contra-tenor, always sustains the Fourth under the Cantus and the upper Third against the Tenor". Accordingly, the Faux-bourdon is nothing else than a series of Sextachords (chords of the Sixth), and although more euphonious, yet not less mechanical, than HUCBALD's "Organum". Its name is explained in various conflicting senses by the writers of the Middle Age; the designation "False Bass" (Faux Bourdon was probably originally applied to the highest voice, for, although the doctrine of the Triad and its inversions was unknown to the musicians of the Middle Age, their ear must have taught them that the Third was by its very nature not adapted to the Bass-leading and belonged properly to the upper voice.* — Other important innovations of the 14th century are: the use of *Syncopation*, by means of which the ear became familiar with the previously tabooed dissonances, as also of the *rests* in the principal melody (Cantus Firmus), which served the double purpose of mitigating the monotony of the constantly repeated chant, and of gaining for the accompanying voices greater freedom of movement. But greatly as the art of polyphonic composition was promoted by all this, yet along side of it *improvised counterpoint* still remained a considerable time in use. This so-called "contrapunto a mente", in which not only one voice but several improvised an accompaniment to the Cantus firmus, must indeed have satisfied higher artistic requirements in exceptional cases only, as the severe criticisms of it by writers on music attest. Supposing, however, a concourse of singers sufficiently gifted and practised — for here, too, certain rules had to be known and observed — to produce an artistically correct polyphony, the performances of these contrapuntists "a mente" certainly appear incomparably worthier of esteem than those of the reproductive artists of our time, who are accustomed to have the composer write out for them not only the notes, but also the embellishments and nuances of the piece to be performed, in which case there can of course be no such thing as reproduction in the higher sense of the word.

The period of the Netherlandic composers, which now follows, beginning with the re-establishment of the Papal chair at Rome (1376), is opened by WILHELM DUFAY, from the Belgian

---

* Altogether different from the above-described Faux-bourdon is the similarly named manner of singing still in use in the Catholic Church, an example of which, among others, is to be found in the celebrated "Miserere" of *Allegri* died 1652. This species of Faux-bourdon consists in a regular four-voiced setting, in which a Gregorian melody is accompanied by three voices in consonances only and in notes of equal value, thus without actual mensural division. Through this extremely simple harmonization the Gregorian Chant was enriched by a new means of expression, without losing its character of sublime simplicity. For the sake of completeness mention must here be made of still a third kind of Faux-bourdon, having, again, nothing in common with the foregoing species, which is simply the execution of a Gregorian melody in the Bass, on the Organ, to which a singer improvises a figured counterpoint.

province of Hennegau, who, probably with many of his countrymen, had followed the Pope from Avignon, and figures in a catalogue of the singers of the Papal chapel in Rome, of the year 1380. He is the first of all mediæval composers whose works show real style. He employs for the first time rests in the middle voices also, whereby melody and voice-leading acquire a certain independence. Here the imitations which MACHAUD only timidly introduced take the form of the *Canon*, then called *Fugue*, from the Latin "fuga" flight, "because" — as the Hamburg musicographer MATTHESON says — "one voice seems to fly away from the other and in that flight is pursued in a pleasant way": whilst by *Canon* was meant a rule for the singer, the summary of the directions for deciphering the mensural notation, which was becoming more and more intricate. The origin of the methods of notation which were in favor with the Netherlandic composers, is to be sought in the fact that the newly acquired art of counterpoint was regarded preeminently as a means of exercising the sagacity of the composer as well as of the performer. Primarily the canonical imitations gave occasion for replacing the notes by signs. In the simple canon it sufficed to give the notation of but one voice, the entrance of the other voices being indicated by a sign. New signs were necessary when it was first permitted to begin the imitating voice in a different pitch from the first voice; moreover, in the canon "by augmentation" and "by diminution", in which the tones of the second voice were to have double or half the length of those of the first. At last there existed so many signs, not strictly belonging to notation, that a composition for many voices, even when these entered *together*, could be written down with but one series of notes, it being left to the sagacity of the performers to divine the composer's intention by means of the annexed signs.[*]

The words of the text were treated by the Netherlandic composers, in their one-sided contrapuntal zeal, with almost no

---

[*] Sometimes the signs were supplied by mysterious texts, as: "Whosoever followeth me, walketh not in darkness", this being a warning to the second voice to pass over the *black notes* of the first. That these aids, too, were occasionally spurned, is proved by a "Kyrie" of the famous OCKENHEIM, which is provided with a sign of interrogation only, and requires the singer to guess not only the entrance of the successive voices, but also the meter, clef and key.

consideration: it sufficed to write down, in a Mass, for instance, the initial words, leaving it to the singer to adapt, in the farther course of the piece, the syllables to the tones as best he could. With this agrees the practice, already mentioned (p. 46), of the mediaeval vocal composers of having in a piece of music two different sets of words sung at the same time, one of sacred, the other of secular character. The origin of this practice is easily shown. The composers, in order to apply their whole skill to the cultivation of the as yet undeveloped polyphonic style, found themselves obliged, before every thing else, to dispense with inventing original themes and to take, as subjects of their pieces, in the principal as well as in the counter voice, exclusively melodies already existing. But to employ, simultaneously with the Gregorian chant a second church-tune as counter voice, was hazardous, as the church had prescribed for each festival a special melody, so that it would be a disturbance of this order to make use of a different church-tune. Thus it came about that for every kind of sacred composition the melody of a *folk-song* was preferably employed for the counter voice. If at the same time the text was left untouched, the reason for this lay entirely in the indifference, already noticed, of composers with regard to the text in general. The reproach of frivolity, on account of such a mixture of the spiritual and the secular, applies as little to them as to the painters, for instance, of the 14th and 15th centuries, who represented in immediate proximity to the Virgin with the Child Jesus the artist's family in the costume of their day. It belonged to the very spirit of the age, that the sacred was not profaned by contact with the secular, rather, on the contrary, that the latter was through the former lifted up and ennobled.

Netherlandic art reaches a second stage of development with OCKENHEIM, born 1430, at Termonde in Flanders, who is rightfully considered the father of counterpoint. With him the *canon* gains in extension and importance, appearing not only in the unison and the octave, but in the fifth and the fourth also. True, OCKENHEIM too carried the contrapuntal subtleties to excess: hence in most of his music labored workmanship is painfully apparent, as, for instance, in a Motet for thirty-six voices, of which latter probably only six or nine were noted, each one taking the form of a canon for six or four voices, which could finally be sung simultaneously. At the same time, we notice in him, as often as he feels himself free from the constraint of polyphony, an ingenious design underlying the composition, and an aspiration after expressive melody.

The achievements of which the Netherlandic counterpoint was capable attained their climax in JOSQUIN DES PRÈS, born 1450, at Condé in the north of France. He is distinguished from his predecessors essentially by the boldness and freedom of his creation: he is the first in the long series of Netherlandic masters to show true geniality in his works. He was not an over-strict follower of the existing rules, as his pupil COCLIUS tells us, though he was thoroughly familiar with them and in his teaching rigidly enforced their observance. As creative musician he certainly made unrestrained use of the prerogative of genius to be a law to itself, and, with his perfect mastery of the forms, his artistic tendency to freedom was an entirely legitimate one. This opinion is expressed by Luther also, who was one of his most ardent admirers, in the following words: "JOSQUIN is a master of the notes; they had to do as he willed, other composers must do as the notes will"; and of his compositions he says: "they are joyous, gentle and lovely, not forced nor constrained and not slavishly tied to the rules, but free as the song of the finch". The pedantry clinging to the Netherlandic school is, to be sure, even in him by no means entirely conquered, and when he gives two musical settings, for instance, of the genealogy of Christ, once according to MATTHEW's gospel, again according to that of LUKE, here, as a matter of course, a genial flight is quite out of the question. On other occasions, however, and even when, according to the fashion of his time, he unites various melodies and texts in the same piece, it is clearly shown by the expressiveness of the musical setting and its adaptation to the poetry, how far he soars above his predecessors. In such cases, moreover, he and his school manifest the endeavor at all events to apply texts agreeing in purport, as for instance in his Dirge on the death of his master OCKENHEIM -- "La déploration de JEAN OCKENHEIM" (given in FORKEL's History of Music, vol. II, p. 512), in which to the "Requiem aeternam" of the tenor four accompanying voices sound in the vernacular, the lament:

> "Nymphes des bois, déesses des fontaines,
> Chantres experts de toutes nations,
> Changez vos voix fort claires et hautaines
> En cris tranchants et lamentations."

As regards the attitude of Josquin's music towards poetry, it is worthy of note that he was the first to recognize, besides the musical, also the esthetic value of the *dissonance* and to apply the latter, consciously and intentionally, to the expression of passionate emotions.

From the period when it had become recognized as the task of the composer to invent not merely artificial tone-combinations but also expressive melodies, the musical mission of the Netherlanders was ended. If the other nations, rightly acknowledging their own inferior talent for it, had left to the Netherlanders alone the development of counterpoint, and also cheerfully conceded to them during a century and a half all the musical honors in the capitals of Europe, they themselves now enter anew upon the musical stage, in the foremost rank the Italians, who soon succeed in gaining for themselves the supremacy in the realm of music. The improvements which just at this time had been made in Italy in the art of multiplying copies of music, likewise contributed in a remarkable degree to the revival of the musical life of the Peninsula. Already in Josquin's time Ottaviano dei Petrucci, named, after his birthplace, a town in the States of the Church, *da Fossombrone*, had invented music-printing with movable metal types. Until then the clumsy wood-cut notes, in vogue since the invention of printing (1440), had had to suffice, or, if elegance of style was required, those artistically ornate copies even now so admired had to be prepared, the possession of which could be afforded only by princely personages or ecclesiastical corporations. This latter case implied of course restriction to one single copy, to be used by several singers at once, whereby, notwithstanding the largeness and plainness of the characters, correct performance was rendered difficult, especially that of polyphonic music, although here the voices were noted down — not *under one another*, as in our scores, but — each one by itself, standing next to each other over the whole surface of the book. Petrucci's editions, the first of which, a collection of 96 three-voiced and four-voiced songs by Netherlandic composers, appeared in the year 1501, remedied all these inconveniences. For beauty and clearness his impressions, judged even by modern standards, leave nothing to be desired, and it is only to be regretted that the works issued by him are printed, after the custom of that time, not in score but in books of single parts, so that the loss of one of these books has in many cases involved that of the whole work.

The transfer of the musical supremacy in favor of Italy which was effected in the course of the 16th century, might seem strange to us if we did not remember that even before this epoch the artistic fecundity of the Italian soil had by no means been dormant. Here, a century earlier, the spirit had been awakened that impelled mankind to search for the lost beauty of antiquity and to be inspired by it to new artistic deeds. The poet-constellation DANTE, PETRARCA and BOCCACCIO had heralded the dawn that now began to brighten the long night of the Middle Age. DANTE shows himself by no means yet emancipated from the views of the scholastic philosophy; in his grand poem of the Last Judgment the Christian theology appears still interwoven with the antique world, and in applying all the wealth of his imagination to present a powerful picture of the all-embracing, all-ruling Roman hierarchy, he reminds us somewhat of those musicians who — as mentioned on page 38 — brought the musical system with all its particulars into symbolical relation to the church. Of one important aid to the knowledge of antiquity DANTE could not avail himself: the Greek language was in his time — he died 1321 — as good as lost, and he had to be satisfied with cultivating his sense for poetic forms through the Latin poets, especially Virgil. More fortunate than he, PETRARCH, the singer of love, had during his sojourn at the papal court at Avignon (1339) enjoyed the opportunity, through the teaching of a resident scholar from Constantinople, to become acquainted with the Greek language, as also with PLATO's works. Lastly, his friend BOCCACCIO (died 1375) had already in his youth acquired a thorough knowledge of the language and science of the Greeks; at his instigation a chair for Greek language and literature was erected in Florence, whose occupant, LEONTIUS PILATUS, undertook to explain to young students for the first time HOMER's poems and PLATO's writings. And how far BOCCACCIO was from scholasticism, with its belief in the exclusive saving power of the Catholic Church, is shown, for example, by the story, given in his "Decameron"* (afterwards reproduced by LESSING in his "Nathan"), of "The Three Rings", which places Christianity, as a not absolutely but only relatively true creed, on an equality with other religions.

The enthusiasm for antiquity kindled by these men was powerfully nurtured by means of the great number of Greek scholars who, after the capture of Constantinople by the Turks (1453), sought refuge in Italy, and were received with open arms not only at the art-loving court of Cosimo dei Medici at Florence, but also at the other seats of culture on the peninsula. To them Europe owed the complete redemption from the intellectual thraldom of the Middle Age, the appearance at last of the day of new birth, of the epoch of the *Renascence*, so important for the advancement of music also; it was to them that SCHILLER, in his poem "The Artists" (Die Künstler) addresses the words:**

> "Ye snatched — when chased Barbarian Hosts before —
> From sacred hearths the last yet living brand;
> From the dishallowed Orient Altar bore,
> And brought it glimmering to the Western Land.
> As from the East the lovely Exile goes,
> Fair on the West a young Aurora glows:
> And all the flowers Ionian shores could yield
> Blush forth, reblooming in the Hesperian Field.
> Fair Nature glassed its image on the soul,
> From the long Night the mists began to roll:
> And o'er the world of Mind, adorned again,
> Light's holy Goddess reassumed her reign."

* A collection of a hundred tales, whose title is compounded from the Greek "deka" ten and "hemera" day, the narration of them being apportioned to ten days.

** The English version is by Sir EDWARD BULWER LYTTON, Bart.

Translator.

V.

LUTHER'S REFORMATION AND THE RENASCENCE.

The revolution of the intellectual life in Europe, brought about through the re-awakening of interest for classical antiquity, affected the domain of music far later than that of poetry and the plastic arts. The reason of this is to be found proximately in the lack of a musical antique; while the poet, as also the painter, the sculptor and the architect met at every step the masterpieces of their predecessors in antiquity, and found in them the stimulus and the pattern for their own creations, to the musician the direct connection with the past was denied. The few relics of ancient Greek music which were discovered at that time could give absolutely no idea of its nature and effect, so that the composer of the period of the Renascence found himself thrown utterly upon his imagination, and the naive, symmetrical beauty of classical antiquity could be at best only of indirect interest to him for his art. A second reason why music remained behind the other arts lay in the external affairs of Italy, in that peculiar medley of rudeness and culture by which precisely the budding-time of the Renascence is characterized. In consequence of the incessant contests between the temporal and the spiritual power a strong, centralized government and a monarchical sentiment had not been able to establish themselves; the sovereign cities and the petty princes were obliged to have not only the interests of science and art but also their material security constantly in view, and under these circumstances it was precisely here that the Middle Age, with its conditions regulated by the law of the strong arm, could be continued longer than elsewhere in Europe. The Italy of the popes JULIUS II. and LEO X. (1503 1513—1521) appears simultaneously *behind* the rest of the world and *in advance* of it: the former as concerns the sense of justice, and respect for property and human life, the latter in regard of the feeling for the beautiful, purity of taste and the initiative in art.

If now, owing to the development of the human body that external laxity brought with it, sculpture and painting could reach that height on which at the time of the above-mentioned popes we see these arts in the works of a LEONARDO DA VINCI, RAPHAEL, MICHAEL ANGELO, the creations of musicians remained unaffected by these influences. It is true that, as we have seen, individual genial natures — JOSQUIN DES PRÈS, for instance — manifested the tendency to expressive composition, thus implying the need of a regeneration of music also; yet on the whole the musical world remains, even after the death of this master (1521), in the bonds of mediaeval restraint. Even at this time the majority of composers continue to neglect the melodic expression and the poetic subject-matter of vocal music in favor of contrapuntal combinations, and as late as the year 1549, thus nearly a century after the Renascence began with the emigration of the Greek scholars expelled from Constantinople, an Italian writer could pronounce the following judgment upon the performances of the papal singers: "They count it their whole joy and their whole merit, that at the same time that one sings "Sanctus" another sings "Sabaoth" and a third, "Gloria tua", and this jumble is accompanied by a howling, a bellowing and growling more resembling the cries of cats in January than the fragrant flowers of May".*

To turn music aside from the narrow tendency given it by the Netherlandic contrapuntists, in order to lead it onward to nobler and higher aims, a stronger impulse was needed than the

---

* As for the first part of this criticism, the neglectful treatment of the text-words, the present age is by no means justified in looking down with disdain upon the performances of the papal singers, as above described; a counterpart to this is found in a much lauded work of the latest music-literature, and indeed, strange to say, in a composer who generally aimed in his vocal music to treat the poetry with more consideration than his predecessors, — in ROBERT SCHUMANN. In the latter's "Faust" music he makes the three female penitents simultaneously sing syllabically different text-words, in which all comprehension of them is of course utterly out of the question.

art-spirit awakened in Italy had been able to give. It was reserved to the Augustinian monk of Wittenberg and subsequently professor Dr. MARTIN LUTHER to succeed, as in the domain of religion so also in that of music, in breaking down the bulwarks of mediaeval tyranny and bringing about the liberation of minds. Through LUTHER's reformation was removed, first of all, the ban resting on church-music since the council of Laodicea, which had directed that the singing at divine service should be committed exclusively to the singers appointed to that end. For, just as protestantism, in opposition to catholicism, made its special aim the intellectual independence of the individual, so too its founder regarded the singing of the congregation as an essential condition of public worship and an effective means of awakening an independent religious sentiment. Accordingly, LUTHER exerted himself personally and with all zeal in improving and ennobling the congregational singing in his church, and with his great musical talent he could himself point out the way in which this end was most quickly to be accomplished. Correctly appreciating the good that catholicism had done for music, he primarily selected from the *ancient Latin church-song* such melodies as were rhythmically like the folk-song and hence specially likely to be caught up by the popular ear. The Gregorian chant (cantus planus) was, as being wholly unrhythmical, rejected by him; LUTHER expresses his aversion to it, on the occasion of a eulogy on polyphonic music, in these words: "Whoever has no love for it (polyphonic music) must in truth be a clumsy blockhead, who does not deserve to hear such delightful music, but only the asinine braying of the Gregorian chant or the singing of dogs or pigs."

As a second source for the reform of congregational singing LUTHER utilized the copious supply of *German spiritual songs* which, even long before the Reformation, had, as constituent part of the liturgy, alternated with the Gregorian chant, especially the songs addressed to the Virgin that had been popularly sung in the 13th century, the words being now altered so as to apply to Christ. He drew, however, still richer material from a third source: the *secular folk-song*, only the music, of course, being utilized. The employment of secular song-melodies for church-tunes had been a common practice from the time of the Netherlandic contrapuntists, and it was therefore doubly natural to make up in this way for the lack of protestant church-tunes.* This transplanting of secular song-tunes into the Church gave offence, to be sure, to the stricter theologians: "what has once been dedicated to the world and Satan" — said they — "should be kept outside of the church". LUTHER, however, was of the opinion that Satan could not be a lover of music and would not begrudge the protestants the theft of his property; unshaken in his conviction that a style of music speaking to the heart of the people must powerfully promote the profounder and purer theory of life aimed at by Protestantism, he proceeded without delay to carry out his plans of musical reform. For all his own thorough and many-sided musical education, he did not disdain the advice and aid of professionals in his work. He summoned to him at Wittenberg JOHN WALTHER, music-director to FREDERICK THE WISE, and in co-operation with him, as also with the Wittenberg singing-master CONRAD RUPFF, produced in 1524 the first protestant hymn-book under the title "Spiritual Song-booklet" (Geystlich Gesangbüchlein), containing 38 German and 5 Latin songs, set for four voices

---

* Very many of the German chorals most renowned for their beauty and devotional character were originally used as humorous songs, love-songs, etc. The practice of adopting secular compositions, such as modern popular songs, pieces from modern operas and instrumental works, to sacred words for use in public worship, has of late years been very common in the United States, and evidently has the approval of the majority of the congregations, especially of those characterized as "fashionable", who are not supposed to take part in the liturgical singing, but delegate this branch of public worship to a paid choir. If, however, in this matter of adapting secular song-tunes to liturgical purposes the rule has been, in more recent times 'otherwise than in Luther's time, to draw the line at *humorous* songs, yet exceptions to this rule are not wanting. One of the most notable of these is the case of a church-tune '? published under the name of "Old Coronation", which, set to the words "All hail the power of Jesus' name", has for many years had an enormous popularity throughout the United States, especially among the so-called "evangelical" sects. This tune was originally composed for an old English pot-house song, some of the stanzas of which are too indecent to print, and certainly, from a musical stand-point the tune is quite worthy of the words. The Germans of LUTHER's day, happily, could utilize for sacred purposes the tunes even of the humorous songs of their time, without incongruity from a musical stand-point, because of the beauty and dignity inherent in those tunes independently of their accidental association with their words. *Translator.*

by WALTHER. It is worthy of notice that here the melody now and then occurs in the upper voice, whereas it had until then always, in polyphonic setting, been sung by the tenor voice. In the course of time the melody became more and more generally allotted to the upper voice; in the last edition of the "Songbooklet" (1551) are found fifty songs arranged in this way, while in the first there are but two.

As to the manner of LUTHER's co-operation in the production of this hymn-book there was for a long time uncertainty. He was credited with the composition of a large number of the melodies contained in it, whereas, according to the latest investigations he can claim the authorship of only three of them, viz: "Ein' feste Burg ist unser Gott", "Jesaias dem Propheten das geschah", and "Wir glauben all' an einen Gott". It should be remembered, in this connexion, that, as in the Middle Age so too in LUTHER's time, the work of the "composer" was divided between two persons: the *inventor* of the melody was not at the same time he who artistically *arranged* it. This division of art-labor may appear to our age as implying a pitiful limitation of powers; yet we should not forget that something similar exists among ourselves, as when the song-composer, *e. g.*, relies for his text upon another person, which to a future generation, possibly again uniting, after the manner of antiquity, the functions of poet and composer in one person, might appear no less pitiful than the mediaeval practice alluded to appears to us.

The effect of the LUTHERAN congregational song was not confined to the protestant church only; its efficacy in promoting the religious life was acknowledged in catholic circles also, and it was even asserted that LUTHER's reform owed its success more to the singing introduced by him than to his doctrine. More grievous than ever appeared now the abuses which, under the sway of the Netherlandic counterpoint, had crept into and established themselves in the artistic music of the Roman church, and the indignation they caused became so great in influential circles, that the cardinals assembled at the *Council of Trent* (1545—1563) seriously raised the question whether the polyphonic or figurate music should not be utterly banished from the church, as detracting from, rather than contributing to, the dignity of the divine service. Meanwhile, however, in PIER LUIGI, called (from his birthplace, near Rome) PALESTRINA,* the master had appeared who was to prove that even the most artistic music is well calculated to move and impress the soul, if only it fulfil the chief requirement of effective vocal music — intelligibility of both melody and words. This condition had already been fulfilled by PALESTRINA in his "*Improperia*" (Reproaches),** published in 1560, a composition in noble and impressive style yet of great simplicity, which aroused such admiration that Pope Pius IV. commanded that they should be included among the compositions intended for the celebration of Holy Week in the Sistine Chapel. Their attention having been thus directed to PALESTRINA, the authorities appointed for reforming the catholic church-music resolved to hazard an additional and final attempt, and commissioned him to produce a composition the success of which should be decisive as to the retention of figurate music in the church. But the three masses thus originated, especially the third, which the composer dedicated to the memory of his patron, pope MARCELLUS II., and called "Missa Papae Marcelli", were found so far superior to the works of previous composers, they so completely satisfied the requisitions made upon genuine church-music, that the judges assembled to decide the question saw their former doubt dispelled at one stroke.

PALESTRINA'S compositions have been called "classic"***, and justly, for the term "classic" is generally applied to an epoch whose artistic products exhibit simple and symmetrical beauty, and, having originated independently of the taste of the day, exert a controlling and refining influence upon all succeeding generations. In this sense we call the palmy days of antique art the "classical" age, and transfer this expression to later times in which

* Pupil of the Netherlander CLAUDIO GOUDIMEL, known as founder of the first public music-schools at Rome 1540, and as musical compiler of the ancient French metrical version of the Psalms, by MAROT and BEZA. GOUDIMEL was killed, as Huguenot, in the massacre of St. Bartholomew's eve, at Lyons, 1572.

** A very solemn part of the service of the Roman Catholic Church for Holy Week, sung on Good Friday, and beginning with the words: "O my people, what have I done unto thee?" etc.   *Translator.*

*** Respecting the origin of the word "classic", it is observed by BRANDE that "The Roman people were divided into classes and the highest order were by prëeminence termed *classici*. Hence the name came to signify the highest and purest class of writers in any language."

the study of the antique is revived. If now the works of modern musical art also cannot claim to be "classical" in the strict sense of the word, because for lack of a musical antique their value cannot be determined in the same manner as is practicable with works of poetry and of plastic art, yet our feeling tells us that also in the musical art-works produced in such times there is an afflatus of classical antiquity. Quite especially do the works of PALESTRINA appear to be filled with the antique spirit of proportion, of conciliation, and of a cheerful beauty, with that spirit which the plastic art of his time had assumed through direct contact with the art-works of antiquity. And though his chord-successions, so strictly conformable to the Gregorian modes, make a strange impression on modern ears, accustomed as they are to the major and the minor mode exclusively, yet the note of artless simplicity characteristic of the works of PALESTRINA and his nearest followers must reveal itself even to those to whom his style — the so-called "Palestrina-style" - - has not yet become familiar.

Almost simultaneously with PALESTRINA's reform of the music of the church begins in Italy a no less successful one in the domain of *secular music*. Here too the polyphonic song perfected by the Netherlanders had attained the exclusive sovereignty: the *Madrigal*, generally a five-voiced secular song (originally Shepherd's-song, from the Italian *Mandriale*, according to some), had become a favorite form of writing with the best composers, especially with LUCA MARENZIO, an attaché of the papal choir (1595—1599), and was regarded as a necessary accompaniment of all occasions, festivals, dramatic performances, and social gatherings, at which the aid of music was required. Although incomparably more expressive and diversified, musically speaking, than the contemporaneous church-music, as was natural, considering the greater freedom of subject-matter and form of the secular poem, yet the Madrigal could no longer satisfy the taste which had become refined in consequence of the study of antiquity. The desire for simpler, more natural vocal music became stronger and stronger, and finally reached in Florence, in a circle of antiquarians, so decided an expression that the members, both amateurs and professional musicians, openly declared war against counterpoint. To substitute for it a kind of music which should, though but proximately, attain the effect of the Greek tragedy-music eulogized by the ancient writers, — this was the pet-idea of the company of men of letters and artists who under the name of *Camerata* (an Italian word corresponding to our English expression "club") regularly met at the house of GIOVANNI BARDI, count of Vernio, for the purpose of artistic entertainment. The first step in this direction was taken by VINCENZO GALILEI, father of the astronomer Galileo Galilei, who, impelled by the discovery of three ancient hymns in the library of the cardinal San Angiolo at Rome,* undertook to compose songs for *one* voice with accompaniment. These songs, whose texts were taken from DANTE's "Inferno" and the "Lamentations of Jeremiah" and which the composer himself executed with viola accompaniment, gained from the members of the Camerata so hearty applause that one of them, the singer GIULIO CACCINI, also determined to devote himself to the new art-species. He went so far in his enthusiasm as to style counterpoint a "laceration" of poetry, and averred that he had made greater advances in his art, through his intercourse with the members of the Camerata than through his previous thirty years' study of counterpoint. As a practical result of these views he published in 1601, under the title *"Nuove Musiche"*, a collection of songs after GALILEI's pattern, and thus brought the new art-species, the *Solo-song* or *Monody*, before the public.

While CACCINI continued to give prominence in his monodies to the lyric and melodic element, soon afterward the Florentine organist and singer, JACOPO PERI, took a farther decisive step towards the realization of the ideal hovering before the minds of the antiquarians, by the invention of an entirely new style of music, which he called *Stile rappresentativo* or *recitativo*. This style, still in use in the opera, occupies the middle ground between song and expressive speech; it was employed by PERI in his music to RINUCCINI's drama, "Dafne", and gained, at the first performance of the work in the circle of the Camerata, the unanimous applause of the hearers. There was a general conviction that the dramatic music of the ancients was now actually re-discovered; and in fact the conditions, the material for re-construct-

---

* These insignificant fragments of Greek music were incapable of affording a foot-hold for new forms, the more so as it was not at that time known even how to decipher them; it was only in the last century that the Frenchman BURETTE succeeded in translating them into modern notation.

ing the ancient music-drama were present: the *Chorus*, for expressing the sentiments of an *ensemble*; the *Arioso*, the melodic song depicting the feelings of the performer, so far as they attain to full expression; and lastly the *Recitative*, for the dialogue and for those sentiments that required only a passing indication.

Emboldened by the success of their work, PERI and RINUCCINI soon after ventured upon a second music-drama, "Euridice", constructed on the same principles, a work destined to form a landmark in the history of music; for the performance of "Euridice" in Florence in 1600, on the occasion of the marriage of Henry IV. of France and Maria de' Medici, ushered into life that art-species which was thenceforth without interruption to occupy the attention of the musical world: *the modern Opera*. The simplicity, not to say meagreness, of both the poetry and the music should not mislead us into underrating the merit of both these dramatic maiden efforts; we should rather, in view of these works, pay to the artistic genius of Italy the tribute of our admiration. CHRYSANDER (Life of Handel, Vol. I.) admits that these achievements of Italian genius would have been impossible to any other nation: "the Florentine Academy, however", says he, "walked upon the clouds of their imagination as upon a paved road, and in the end attained what they had proposed to themselves to reach."

A closer inspection of the new art-species reveals, it is true, a very great difference between it and its Greek prototype. In regard of its relation to public life and civilization, as also to the ideas conditionating its existence, it remained as far from the antique tragedy as we can possibly conceive. Born — not of religious conceptions, but — of courtly luxury, the opera became for the time being a *monopoly of princes and the great*, and even if the populace were here and there admitted to it, it could have no intelligent comprehension of the subject-matter, drawn as it was exclusively from ancient mythology and heroic legend. Not till long afterwards could the opera abandon this exclusive standpoint and acquire significance for the culture-life of the masses, although not, even then, in the sense of its antiquity-loving founders. That, notwithstanding, the labor of the Florentine camerata was by no means thrown away, that on the contrary the seed sown by it was even in the course of the next decennium to bear abundant fruit, will be seen in the next section.

VI.

ITALIAN OPERA.

The first important step in its march of development was taken by the new art-species discovered by the Florentines — the modern opera, then styled *Dramma in musica*, or *Tragedia per musica* — not at the place of its birth, but at Venice. Here ADRIAN WILLAERT (pronounced *Willart*), one of the last, but also of the greatest, of the Netherlandic composers (born 1490, at Bruges, died 1563), had founded a school, whose influence was in no wise diminished even after the withdrawal of the Netherlanders from the musical supremacy. He had striven, with even greater success than his countryman JOSQUIN, to make the art of tone serviceable to musical thought, especially to animate the polyphonic forms by means of dramatic expression. The very external surroundings of the city could not but exert a stimulating influence in this direction upon the musician. As a securely isolated commercial republic, Venice had had little or nothing to suffer from the oppression of the church and the political disturbances that had impeded the rest of Italy in its development, and far earlier here than there the thought could be entertained of giving art and science a share in social life. Through the commercial relations with the East there were brought to the city, in addition to material prosperity, manifold elements of culture also, which, blended with the indigenous ones, gave it that motley, fantastic character which manifests itself with so special prominence in the works of its architects and painters. But the musician, in the midst of a population given up to the cheerful, unconstrained enjoyment of life, would naturally feel with double force the prosiness of the mediaeval art-music, and zealously aim to bring the art of tone nearer to the general comprehension. In this WILLAERT succeeded by an extremely simple means: the peculiar architectural proportions of the church of San Marco, of which he was music-director, with its two galleries, each provided with an organ, gave him the idea of dividing his choral masses, in order to unravel, as far as possible, the entangled polyphonic texture. The perfect success of this attempt led him afterwards to utilize also the smaller side-galleries of the church for placing separate groups of singers. To WILLAERT therefore may be justly ascribed the origin of the principle of what is called the *double choir* or *chorus*.

With WILLAERT his most eminent pupils CYPRIAN DE RORE and GIOSEFFO ZARLINO shared in the musical renown of Venice during the Cinquecento — as the Italians call, by way of abbreviation (instead of *Mille cinquecento* = 1500), the period of the Renascence. The former, by birth a Netherlander, yet thoroughly under the musical influence of Italy, made an additional advance in the direction inaugurated by his master, by enhancing in a remarkable manner the capacity of music for *expression* by means of free use of the *chromatic* element. In his "Chromatic Madrigals", published in 1544, the severe diatonic character of the church-modes is, by frequent use of the chromatic half-step and of the consequent augmented and diminished intervals, utterly annulled, an innovation which, no less successful than WILLAERT's system of divided choirs, contributed to the liberation of music from the tyranny of ecclesiastical ordinances and to its invigoration for the solution of higher art-problems. — The latter, ZARLINO (born 1517, at Chioggia, near Venice), the first Italian to attain, side by side with the Netherlanders, a high musical rank, was influential chiefly through his theoretical works, of which some, especially his principal work, "Istituzioni harmoniche", published in 1557, have attained the honor of marking an epoch. For, although he was greatly celebrated by his contemporaries as composer also, and appears — *e. g.*, in his "Modulationes sex vocum", posthumously published at Venice, 1566 — as a composer of distinguished ability, yet his merits in this domain are far behind those which he acquired, as theorist, in elucidating the intricacies that in his time still inhered in musical science. The maxims and doctrines enunciated by him in the above-mentioned "Istituzioni harmoniche", and still farther developed in the subsequently published "Dimostrazioni harmoniche" and "Sopplimenti musicali", not only opened new careers to the musicians of his time, but have also been recognized by all later generations as the sure foundation of musical theory and practice.

One particular in which ZARLINO's agency was of wide-spreading importance, is that he took a decisive step in the improvement of the *musical temperament*, which, with the increasing cultivation of polyphonic vocal and instrumental music, had become an imperative necessity. By *temperament* is understood the determination of certain deviations from the natural measurement of the intervals, which determination is necessary in order that the intervals may in all possible melodic and harmonic inter-relationships be euphonious, as being — to use the technical expression — "in tune": in other words, in order to adapt them to the limits of the Octave, as determined by the nature of the human vocal organs, which limits they in their natural measurement either fall short of or exceed.[*] Up to ZARLINO's time the accepted system had been that of PYTHAGORAS, which consisted of *perfect*[**] *Fifths*. The *Third* employed was that resulting from a fourth upper Fifth, as: c, g, d, a, e, — where e forms the Third to c. This so-called *Pythagorean Third*, as being too *sharp* for a consonance, was counted as a *dissonance*. ZARLINO established the system named after him sometimes called the *pure diatonic system*, of which one of the most important features, practically, was the reduction of the Third by a minute interval ("comma"), thus enabling the Third to rank as *consonance*. And whereas composers had till then shunned the Third in the opening and the closing chord of their works, the *Triad*, the true basis of all polyphonic music, could now enter into its kingdom — for the time being, of course, only the *major* Triad. As for the *minor* Third, it was not yet

---

[*] See, on the subject of "Temperament", Sedley Taylor's "Science of Music", Chapter X, my "Primer of Modern Musical Tonality", Chap. VI, etc.
Translator.

[**] Perfect, that is, in the *acoustic* sense, not in the sense in which the term has (unfortunately, as I think) so long been applied to a species of Fifth more appropriately styled, by advanced modern music-theorists, *major*. See my "Primer", above cited, *Note*, p. 53. *Translator.*

regarded as a consonance: for centuries long it was considered better to end a composition in minor with a *major* Triad, even at the sacrifice of unity of mode, than to introduce the minor Third in the final chord.

To return to the subject of the Opera, it is to be especially noticed that a particularly favorable soil for its cultivation had been prepared by the antecedent labors of the masters above-mentioned. Through WILLAERT and his school the Venetian church-music had acquired that dramatic and highly-colored character that later also, under his successors ANDREA GABRIELI and his nephew GIOVANNI, distinguished it from the other Italian schools, and it was inevitable that the new-born music-drama also should be materially influenced in its development by this feature. Precisely a half-century after WILLAERT's death we again find in the place that had been filled by him a musician through whom opera received an impulse hardly dreamed of by its inaugurators: CLAUDIO MONTEVERDE (born at Cremona in 1568, and from 1613 till his death in 1643 music-director of the church of San Marco). Even before his call to Venice, as music-director at Mantua this artist had exerted himself to augment the musical means of description and of representing strongly agitated states of mind, first, by the very free use of *dissonances** previously prohibited, then by a judicious treatment of the orchestra, after he had recognized the *individuality of the several instruments* and their adaptability for characterising the *dramatis personæ* and the various situations. In one of his "Martial Madrigals", for instance, the four bowed-instruments accompanying the recitative take a lively part in the effective representation of the contest; here, too, appears for the first time the violin-tremolo, for strengthening, in the proper place, the impression of the violent and passionate — a style of

---

* MONTEVERDE did not hesitate to let the Dominant-seventh, the Ninth, even the major Fourth (Tritone) enter unprepared, and that in the outer voices; moreover he is the first to use the diminished Septimachord, — daring innovations, which drew upon him savage attacks from the theorists, especially from ARTUSI, of Bologna, who said of him, among other things, "that he lost sight of the proper aim of music, viz: to give pleasure". In our own days a school of estheticians ably represented by the late eminent critic Dr. EDUARD HANSLICK, teach substantially the same doctrine, as opposed to *modern* innovations. Thus history repeats itself. *Translator.*

execution that was received at first with censure and ridicule, but soon became general and has existed to this day.

Naturally, opera was to be the proper field for MONTEVERDE's activity: he did not, however, turn his attention to it before the year 1607, when he brought out, on the occasion of a festival at the court of Duke GONZAGA of Mantua, his dramatic maiden-essay, "Orfeo", the text by RINUCCINI. This was followed the year after by the "Arianna", and the dance-opera "Il ballo delle ingrate". In Venice he then wrote a series of operas; and to the period of his activity in that city belongs an important event for the progress of the music-drama, of which he must be regarded as the immediate instigator, the establishment of the *first opera-house*, in consequence of which the opera lost its character as exclusively court-festivity and became accessible to the general public. It was in Venice that in the year 1637 the first opera-house, the *Teatro Cassino*, was opened, the opera being the "Andromeda", the text by FERRARI, the music by MANELLI. Some years afterward the theatre San Moïse was opened with MONTEVERDE's newly studied "Arianna", and in the course of the same century opera in Venice received such an impulse that (as Marpurg narrates) up to 1727 fifteen operatic enterprises were set on foot by private means, and up to 1734 some four hundred operas by forty different composers were performed.

Of MONTEVERDE's successors CAVALLI (music-director at the San Marco church from 1668) is the only one who can be said to have farther developed the dramatic style; the celebrity of this composer, moreover, was not confined to his native country, as is proved by his call to Paris to produce his opera "Xerxes" on the occasion of the wedding of Louis XIV. After him Italian opera gradually diverges from the path originally taken, and sacrifices the antique simplicity aimed at by its founders to the ever increasing demand for sensuous charm. The alliance of poetry and music, dissolved in the Middle Age and renewed but a few decennaries before, is again broken off, and the equilibrium that had just been acquired is sacrificed anew to the claims of music. Nevertheless, the period that now ensues can be called the palmy days of Italian opera: the musical leadership in Italy, hitherto taken in turn by Rome, Florence and Venice, is now assumed by a fourth city, NAPLES, and ALESSANDRO SCARLATTI (died 1725, as music-director at that court) is the composer that determines for opera the course of development it has now to pursue. The bright sky of Naples and the gay disposition of its inhabitants had, it is true, at an earlier period brought to maturity a rich musical harvest on the soil of the ancient Greek colony, but far less in the domain of serious music than in that of the secular song, the madrigal, which — not to mention other names — the highly gifted amateur and art-patron CARLO GESUALDO, prince of Venosa died 1614), cultivated to a high degree of perfection. But with SCARLATTI the musical tendencies of the Neapolitans began to reveal themselves in so brilliant and extensive a manner as to allow the formation here of a distinct musical style adapted to the local surroundings, called, because of its melodic charms, the *beautiful style*, in distinction to the Roman style of PALESTRINA and his school, called the *sublime*.

ALESSANDRO SCARLATTI himself sprang from the Roman school of CARISSIMI, celebrated for his promotion of chamber-music and the oratorio, of whose agency in the latter domain we shall speak later. With regard to the *chamber-music style* developed by him, which exercised a considerable influence on the art-tendency of the Neapolitan school, be it here observed that it is distinguished from the church-style by its very nature as secular, but from the dramatic style, which conformably to its character depicts the emotions with heavy powerful touches, and for reaching its larger circle of hearers aims at simplicity and intelligibility, by a far more detailed artistic exploitation and development of the musical thought. Careful and fine work of this kind is the more necessary in the chamber-music style, as here the attention is not exacted either by external representation, as in dramatic music, nor by religious ceremonies, as in church-music, hence concentrates itself entirely upon the musical work; because, moreover, in chamber-music there is but one player to a part, and here therefore the tone-masses, dynamic effects and color-shadings obtainable in orchestral music are not to be expected. Besides CARISSIMI, another pupil of the Roman school, AGOSTINO STEFFANI (called as music-director to Hanover in 1685) notably contributed to the development of the chamber-music style. As dramatic composer of comparatively little significance he indirectly promoted purity of style in dramatic music through his *Chamber-duets*, in which species he has produced model works.

Trained in the strict school of chamber-music to be a composer, SCARLATTI had now become capable of laboring successfully in every special department of his art; and though his chief merit lies in the promotion of dramatic music, yet so noteworthy were his contributions to the church and the chamber also, that they served even a HANDEL as models, and were no less eagerly studied by him than his operas. His fertility was almost incredible: in the year 1721 — four years before his death — he had already finished his 114th opera, and his 200th mass, while the number of his cantatas — little musical dramas, as Fétis calls them — is incalculable. Dr. BURNEY discovered an original manuscript of his containing 35 Cantatas (composed in 1701 at Tivoli, where SCARLATTI was visiting a colleague of the papal chapel), each bearing date of the following day. In his operas he unites the richness of melody and the dramatic forcefulness of the southern Italians with the gravity and the purity of style of the Roman art-song: they are characterised rather by pleasing and simple melodies than by strong passionate expression, yet he can excellently depict situations, especially comic ones. His forms are still extremely narrow in comparison to those of the later Neapolitans and of HANDEL and BACH, yet they served for a long time as models, especially the forms of the *Aria* and the *Overture*; the latter is, like that introduced by LULLI in France, in three parts, and differs from the French in this only, that its opening and closing parts are in quick, the middle part in slow, *tempo*, whereas in the French form a lively middle part is enclosed between two middle parts.*

Not only as composer did ALESSANDRO SCARLATTI powerfully influence the taste of his time and of the generation following: he was, besides — as were usually the song-composers of the

---

* The SCARLATTI overture may be regarded as the prototype of the modern *orchestral symphony*. As instrumental music became more and more independent, the opera-overture, enlarged in form and enriched in subject-matter, began to be utilized for concert-purposes; afterwards its three parts were separated and became independent movements, to which in the 18th century a fourth one was added, by the transfer of the Minuet from the ancient Suite.

preceding centuries — an excellent singer and singing-teacher, moreover a genial conductor, finally an accomplished player of the clavicembalo — the piano-forte of those days (although excelled in this respect, as we are told, by his son DOMENICO, whose significance for instrumental music will be discussed elsewhere). Thus SCARLATTI could fruitfully labor in all departments of his art, especially as teacher of students of music everywhere, bitterly attacked though he was by the theorists of his time for his daring use of musical resources. And as in every age we see the artistically productive contemporaries of a pioneer genius follow, consciously or unconsciously, the path he has taken, so too SCARLATTI'S style became, even during his life-time, the pattern for the creations of the rising generation, and afterwards, completely developed by his pupils LEONARDO LEO and FRANCESCO DURANTE, attained the supremacy over all musical Europe. Like the Netherlanders in the 15th and 16th centuries, the Neapolitans now exercised an almost unlimited influence upon the musical affairs of the civilized world. Even in France, where, about the middle of the 17th century, a peculiar kind of music-drama, in keeping with the national art-ideas, had developed itself, there was an opposition party that received with open arms the Neapolitan opera appearing about the middle of the 18th century, and was powerful enough to combat with temporary success, under the direction of the Neapolitan PICCINI, the French opera represented by GLUCK. In England Italian opera had from the end of the 17th century got a footing and overcome the rivalry of both French and native composers; but during the palmy days of the Neapolitan school it was strong enough to drive from the field a musician of HANDEL'S power and standing, as is proved by the success of the London opera at the Haymarket theatre under the direction of PORPORA and HASSE, at the expense of HANDEL'S opera in Coventgarden theatre.

In Germany, Vienna, Dresden and Berlin strove with equal zeal to naturalize Italian opera among themselves. The most prominent musicians here were, it is true, mostly German by birth, but in their musical education and activity thoroughly italianized; for instance, JOHANN JOSEPH FUX, who, as chief music-director to three German emperors, with the aid of his sub-directors the Venetians CONTI and CALDARA, in the first half of the 18th century brought the Vienna opera to an extraordinary height of excellence, and at the same time proved, by his famous work on counterpoint — "Gradus ad Parnassum" — published in 1745, that his association with Italian opera had not cost him his German thoroughness. Of equal importance for Dresden was JOHANN ADOLPH HASSE, born in 1699 near Hamburg, from 1724 on in Naples as pupil of SCARLATTI and PORPORA, eventually, after brilliant successes in Italy, appointed music-director at the court of Saxony; for Berlin, CARL HEINRICH GRAUN, born 1701, till his death in 1759 sole director of the Italian opera established by Frederick the Great on his accession to the throne.

A characteristic feature of the music of this century is the perfecting of the musical means of expression, especially of artistic singing. As the father of the Neapolitan school, ALESSANDRO SCARLATTI, was an excellent singer, so his successors also. Artistic singing was the school through which every composer had to go before he might hope for any success whatsoever for his productions. HASSE began his career as tenor at the Hamburg opera-house, GRAUN also belonged to the representatives of the art of finished singing, and was enabled, as such, to win during his residence in Italy the applause of all critics. The Italian art of singing reached its climax in the school established by PISTOCCHI at Bologna about 1700, of whose successful activity the singers at the London opera in HANDEL's time give splendid testimony, notably the male soprano SENESINO and the female singers CUZZONI and FAUSTINA HASSE. But the reverse side of virtuosity, pride and boundless vanity, manifests itself in these singers in the most disagreeable manner. CUZZONI was, we are told, a veritable dragon in character, and when HANDEL, to manage her better, had called to London her artistic equal, HASSE's wife, the quarrel between the two artistes soon became so violent that on one occasion they came to blows on the open stage.

But the more highly the performances of the song-virtuosi were esteemed and remunerated by the public — as early as 1647 the Roman musicographer Doni could testify that "they lived in such luxury that each one of them had more than ten cantors and choir-masters could earn" — all the lower was the estimation in which the composer was held. In the opera of the 18th century the music was judged almost exclusively according to the opportunity it afforded the singer to display his or her virtuosity: "notably the *aria* was in its first part (repeated at the close) as it were merely the lattice-work which the singer decorated with all possible arabesques and graces into a little triumphal arch for himself".* If dramatic music was able subsequently to come out of the fight against virtuosity triumphant and re-enforced, for another branch of musical art this precarious state of things became utterly fatal: church-music in the course of the 18th century steadily declined; the grave and dignified style of DURANTE, founder of the newer Neapolitan school (died in 1755, as music-director at the conservatory of San Onofrio at Naples), is exchanged by his successors for the showy secular style or a romantic unrest. This is seen, *e. g.*, in PERGOLESE's "Stabat mater", the music of which, predominantly sensuous as it is and made to depend for its effect chiefly on the charm of the voice, only partially deserves the praises bestowed upon it by contemporaries. JOMELLI is the only one among the later Italians in whose church-music the gravity and thoroughness of the Roman school are still effective, properties that are predominant in his later works, most likely in consequence of his residence in Germany (1754—1765 as music-director at Stuttgart, at the court of Duke Charles of Würtemberg.

Even at the time when the musical genius of Germany is awakened, when with GLUCK and MOZART dramatic music takes an unexpectedly lofty flight, even then Italian opera by no means owns itself defeated, and continues to achieve brilliant successes. In Paris PICCINI manages to maintain for many years a respectable position side by side with GLUCK; in Vienna at the time of MOZART's greatest celebrity the Neapolitans PAISIELLO and SARTI obtain enthusiastic applause, the former by his opera "Barbiere di Seviglia", the latter by his "Due litiganti", which together with VINCENZO MARTIN's "Cosa rara" is utilized by MOZART in the second finale of his "Don Giovanni". Even the appearance of the phenomenon BEETHOVEN could not prevent Europe from repeating in our century its surrender at discretion to Italian opera. ROSSINI (born 1792, at Pesaro in the states of the church) was the magician who was able, by means of the sensuous charm of Italian melody, to captivate anew the musical world that had

---

* See VON DOMMER's *Manual of Music-history*.

been educated to a higher intelligence by the Viennese masters. From 1813, when his "Tancred" was given in Venice for the first time, till the appearance of his last work, "William Tell", in 1829 at the Grand Opera in Paris, Rossini's musical career was signalized by a series of triumphs such as no Italian opera-composer before him had enjoyed. This was owing, in the first place, to his creative power, which manifests itself not only in melodic invention but also in a novel — for his time — treatment of harmonies and of the orchestra; farthermore to the vocal skill at his disposal, and this especially after the impresario BARBAJA had, in 1815, engaged him and the elite of Italy's male and female singers to bring out his works in Naples, Milan and Vienna alternately. Finally, the political circumstances also must be taken into consideration to account for the enthusiasm called forth by the appearance of the Rossini opera: the mental enervation that had settled upon Europe after the disturbances attendant upon the wars of Napoleon, and the consequent need of means of diversion and stupefaction. "From the days of the Vienna Congress", says RIEHL ("Musikalische Charakterköpfe"), "from the decennium, sultry, truce-bidding, flood-gate-erecting, that followed the war of deliverance, dates ROSSINI's world-wide fame. The weary nations required lullabies by which to go to sleep and dream, and the Italian offered them the sweetest, most voluptuous slumber-song. Every one was tired of the bombastic, tragic pathos of the Napoleonic school, on the stage as well as in life; it was desired to drink sweet oblivion at the spring of diverting art, and where was art more diverting than in the ROSSINI opera?"

The exclusiveness with which part of the musical world gave itself up to the enjoyment of ROSSINI's operas, and indeed even to that degree that the greatest German masters, BEETHOVEN and WEBER, were placed, at the very posts of their personal activity, in the background as compared with the "swan of Pesaro" — this exclusiveness excited in the circles of music-lovers with higher aims an aversion to Italian opera-music in general, which likewise was carried to excess and led to unjust depreciation of its value. Later Italian opera-composers, as BELLINI and DONIZETTI, were, by reason of the cloying sweetness of their melodies and the meagreness of their harmonies and rhythm, not adapted to diminish that aversion.* The very latest phase of Italian opera-music, as represented by GIUSEPPE VERDI (born 1813, at Busseto, near Parma) in his "Aïda", seems to indicate a tendency to break with the traditional style, in so far as this style is characterized chiefly by the predominance of melodic forms adapted principally to the display of solo vocalism, in accordance with the genius of the Italian people, and by general harmonic and rhythmic poverty and lack of dramatic truthfulness.

---

* What follows of this Section is substituted for considerably more matter in the original, which, as being concerned mostly with what the author considers the unjust prejudices of his countrymen against Verdi and Italian opera generally, I judged would not specially interest English-speaking readers.
Translator.

VII.

FRENCH OPERA.

In no nation of Europe could the example given by Italy of the renovation of the musical drama of the ancients more powerfully excite emulation than in the French, whose inclination to music, as no less to dramatic representation, had already in the Middle Age been variously manifested, and through the artistic current of the 16th century had received fresh nourishment. Even during the political and religious disturbances of this period the Renascence was able here to exercise its wholesome influence upon the art-situation. But after the religious schisms and the attendant civil wars had, in consequence of the edict of Nantes (1598), reached their termination, and after RICHELIEU's iron hand had broken the resistance of the nobility and restored the national unity, the artistic impulses of the French people could, side by side with material prosperity, so freely develop themselves that the nation soon came up with the start gained by the Italians in the intellectual domain.

The first one to satisfy the demand for a reform of the French drama in the modern sense was a Venetian named BAIF, who in 1570 solicited from CHARLES IX. a privilege for the erection of an academy for dramatic poetry and music, and obtained it, but was prevented by the unfavorable circumstances of the times from carrying out his design. Under the reign of the pleasure-loving king HENRY IV. these musico-dramatic plans might perhaps have been realized, had his beneficial activity not been brought by RAVAILLAC's dagger (1610) to an unexpectedly sudden close. HENRY's successor, LOUIS XIII. was, on account of his gloomy disposition, not inclined to offer to the arts an asylum at his court: but this very circumstance was to be the occasion of the first appearance of opera in France, inasmuch as the Cardinal MAZARIN, in order to enliven Queen ANNE OF AUSTRIA, sent for an Italian opera-troupe to come to Paris, which, in 1645, in the Salon du Petit Bourbon opened their performances with the opera "La finta pazza", composed by STROZZI.

The applause that the new art-species earned at the hands of the French public could be only a partial one, as opera had at this time considerably receded from the noble simplicity originally aimed at, and sought for effect almost exclusively in externals, in richness of decorations, of costumes and of ballets, in which last for variety's sake all imaginable animal forms figured. But this could not satisfy a nation whose taste for dramatic poetry had, by men like CORNEILLE, whose "Cid" had appeared as early as 1636, and MOLIÈRE, who had begun his career at Paris in 1644, been in a remarkable degree purified and polished. Accordingly, the desire was openly expressed to see the music-drama which had been introduced from Italy transformed in a manner corresponding to the national art-ideas. What seemed to be an insuperable obstacle to the fulfilment of this desire was the established opinion in the literary circles of France that the French language was not adapted for being joined with music. In fact, it had since the reforms of the writer and poet MALHERBE (1555—1628) been limited to so strict forms, in poetry the Alexandrine verse had attained so absolute a supremacy, that to the vocal composer the free, independent movement of his fantasy was rendered almost impossible. As, at the time of the Netherlandic contrapuntists, poetry had been subordinate to music, now in France the situation was reversed. A freer treatment of the language seemed to be the indispensable requirement for calling to life a national opera: a poet must be found courageous enough to disregard the existing rules, and this was the Abbé PERRIN, who accordingly deserves to be mentioned in the first rank among the founders of French opera.

Little as PERRIN could stand comparison, in point of poetic talent, with the poet-heroes of his time, yet in compensation he possessed in a high degree the dramatic experience necessary for carrying out his plan, inasmuch as the court of Gaston, DUKE OF ORLEANS, brother of LOUIS XIII., at which he filled the office of master of ceremonies, was, in perfect contrast with the court of the misanthropic monarch, the theatre of every kind of amusement, histrionic especially. Here the Abbé conceived the idea of a style of poetry which, by means of new and irregular forms, as also by the expression of manifold emotions, should be calculated to excite the fantasy of the musician. His poems written on this principle and after the pattern of the so-called "versi sciolti" (blank verse) of the Italians, which he published in 1661 as verses for music, naturally excited the most violent opposition of the professional poets, at the head of whom was BOILEAU, afterwards author of the work named after HORACE's "Ars poetica", "L'art poëtique". All the more thankfully were they received by musicians, and the most noted composer of the France of that time, ROBERT CAMBERT, organist of the church of St. Honoré and musical intendant to the queen-mother, indicated his readiness to accept PERRIN's innovations in the preface to a collection of his drinking-songs, in which he expresses the hope "that the beauty of the words may atone for the defects of the music, they being written mostly by Monsieur PERRIN, as to whose incomparable talent for writing musical texts there is no dispute". With this composer PERRIN united in carrying out his musico-dramatic reformatory plans, and the first fruit of their joint labor was a vaudeville entitled "Pastorale, première comédie française en musique", first performed in 1659 at the castle of the farmer-general de la Haye, at Issy, near Paris.

The brilliant success of this undertaking was especially creditable to the poet and the composer for the reason that both had disdained to employ on this occasion the customary external means of producing effect, and thus the applause showered on the work was aimed at its intrinsic worth exclusively. Nevertheless, years had to pass before French opera could take one step in advance of the first stage of infancy. In the first place, PERRIN had to put up with the disappointment of seeing an Italian opera — CAVALLI's "Xerxes", already mentioned — chosen for the marriage-celebration of Louis XIV., although his own "Pastorale" had, shortly after its performance at Issy, been brought out before the court at Vincennes and obtained a favorable reception. But this disappointment availed as little as the death of his patrons — first, of the DUKE OF ORLEANS, then of Cardinal MAZARIN —

to hinder the enterprising poet in the energetic prosecution of the work he had begun. By unremitting exertions and petitions he succeeded, in 1699, thus fully ten years after the first representation of the "Pastorale", in getting a royal patent, granting to him for twelve years the exclusive right to establish in Paris and all other cities of the kingdom "Opera-academies after the manner of the Italian ones."* He now formed an association with CAM-BERT, the MARQUIS OF SURDÉAC and a certain CHAMPERON, on which latter the supervision of the decoration and the financial management devolved: the best vocal talent of the kingdom as also the royal ballet-master, BEAUCHAMP, as "chef de la danse", were secured for the undertaking, and soon a suitable place was found for erecting a theatre. At the end of five months the new building was erected on the site of the "Jeu de paume de la bouteille" (tennis-court in the Rue Mazarin, and in 1671 was opened with the opera "Pomona", a work which in regard of both the music and the poetry was far inferior to the maiden effort of PERRIN and CAMBERT, yet had such an attraction for the public that it had a run of fully eight months and brought into the poet alone the sum of 30.000 francs ($ 6.000).

Meanwhile a dangerous rival to the youthful enterprise had grown up in the person of GIOVANNI BATTISTA LULLY** or LULLI, who, born in Florence in 1633, came to Paris as a boy and gradually worked his way up from a scullion to Mademoiselle DE MONT-PENSIER, niece of the king, to a favorite of LOUIS XIV. Dismissed in disgrace by his mistress in consequence of a satirical poem upon her, he first obtained through his talent for the violin employment in the royal orchestra, the "grande bande" of twenty-four "violons du roy": after he had there attracted the king's attention, a special orchestra of sixteen musicians was formed for him, called the "petits violons", in distinction to the older and more numerous orchestra. Finally he managed as play-actor also to ingratiate himself with the king and to render his favor secure

---

* "Diverses Académies, dans lesquelles il se fait des représentations en musique, qu'on nomme opéra" sic . The designation "Académie royale de Musique", to this day with occasional change of the word "royale" into "impériale" or "nationale" the official name of the Paris so-called "Grand Opera", appears only after PERRIN'S patent had passed over to his successors.

** Properly written "Lulli", as there is no "y" in the Italian alphabet.

by his irresistible drollery, as often as his position at court seemed to be imperilled. Trusting to the partiality of the powerful sovereign he conducted himself, for more quickly attaining his ends, towards the public as also towards his colleagues with the utmost want of consideration. As he had most grievously injured and offended the most eminent men of his time — BOILEAU, LA-FONTAINE, and even MOLIÈRE, to whose friendly advances he owed his first successes, — so now, made jealous by the success of the PERRIN-CAMBERT undertaking, he did not hesitate to apply every means of intrigue in order to rob these two men of the fruits of their labor. And in this he succeeded in the year 1672, when he availed himself of a quarrel that had broken out between the four directors of the enterprise, to transfer to himself the patent granted to PERRIN, and thus became the master of the whole domain of French opera. Vain were the protestations of the victims of this robbery: PERRIN's complaints were unheeded, and after a year's time his name was no longer mentioned. CAMBERT too had to acknowledge that by the side of LULLI there was no place for him: he removed to London, but, despite his brilliant successes there as composer, could not forget the mishap he had experienced in his native country, and died a few years afterwards (1677), poisoned by LULLI, as the enemies of the latter maintained.

With LULLI begins the true golden age of grand opera in France, seeing that he had rightly estimated the public need of a music-drama corresponding to the national sentiment, and was perfectly able to satisfy it. PERRIN's attempt to shake off the constraint of the poetic forms could, in view of the belief of the French in the immutability of certain dogmas, not possibly have a thorough success: it had come too late to turn back the previously mentioned development of the language. LULLI, on the contrary, conformed strictly to the dominant art-views, and the eminence that he attained among the French people as opera-composer is due not so much to his musical talent as to his ability to enter into the essential nature of tragedy, according to the representations that the French had formed to themselves of this art-species. "As the French drama", says VON DOMMER (History of Music), "sought to conform itself to the laws of the ancient Greek Drama, so LULLI, too, in his music stood far nearer to the ideas of its nature in the antique music-drama than did the contemporaneous Italians, among whom music had, in opera also, emancipated itself from Greekism and struck out a path for itself." As musical art-works Lulli's operas are inferior to those of the Italians of that time. With him the centre of gravity lies in the musical rhetoric and declamation, in the dramatic expression, which he aims at by the close union of tone with speech; and accordingly, his musical forms are simple, not to say meagre, as compared with the broadly developed tone-forms of the contemporaneous Italian opera, destructive though this development must be admitted to be, for the most part, of dramatic truthfulness. This weak side of Lulli's operas is, however, compensated by his exact knowledge of the stage, as also by his ability to make a skilful use of all external theatrical appliances. To this must be added the earnestness with which he set about to accomplish what he had found to be right and necessary. Just as he tyrannized outrageously over his poet Quinault, and struck out from and added to his works till they perfectly accorded with his intentions, so too, when his operas were being studied he kept the singers, the chorus, the orchestra and the dancers to their task with a painful exactness. Especially he exerted himself to impart to his actors better stage-manners, a higher degree of mimetic skill, and a more distinct enunciation of the words — the latter being an essential condition of the success of his music, whose declamatory character is never disavowed, not even in the choruses, which participate far more extensively in the dramatic action than the Italian opera-chorus, and thus on their part also demonstrate the affinity of the French opera with the antique tragedy. From all this it is easily understood why Lulli's works were not only held in great esteem by the French public during his life-time, but could also after his death (1678) hold their ground upon the stage nearly a whole century long. It was not till the year 1774 that they disappeared from the operatic repertory, simultaneously with the appearance of Gluck's "Iphigenia in Aulis", whose reform of the musical drama, moreover, substantially follows the principles of Lulli, just as the latter have also remained up to the present time the standard for the French grand opera.

There was but one composer who could during this long period put himself abreast of Lulli: Jean Philippe Rameau (born

1683, at Dijon). The superior of his predecessor as musician, he notably enriched French opera-music from the melodic and the harmonic side, yet without sacrificing the dramatic to the musical element and thus becoming disloyal to the principles followed by Lulli. It was not till comparatively late, in his fiftieth year, that Rameau began his career as opera-composer; but as he had during the first and greater half of his artist-life been uninterruptedly employed with music — with what success is proved by what he accomplished as theoretician and as piano-virtuoso and composer for this instrument —, he could already at the appearance of his first opera "Hippolyte et Aricie" (October 1st, 1732) develop an epoch-marking activity in the dramatic domain also. Even here is seen the difference between his talent and that of Lulli: the latter retains from the first to the last of his operas the same musical method, whereas in Rameau's works the richest variety reigns, with an endeavor to employ constantly new means of expression and to render the style diversified. The exuberance of musical thoughts by which in the above-mentioned opera he surprised his contemporaries and at first (as may be imagined) puzzled them, justifies the opinion expressed by the esteemed composer Campra (from 1722 till his death in 1744 music-director to Louis XV.), "that 'Hippolyte et Aricie' contained matter enough for ten ordinary operas, and that Rameau would eclipse all the masters of his time". At first the artist had of course to suffer the most violent attacks from the public: the blind adherents of Lulli especially could not forgive him his innovations and revenged themselves on him by the following epigram, among other things:

> Si le difficile est le beau,
> C'est un grand homme que Rameau.
> Mais si le beau, par aventure
> N'était que la simple nature,
> Quel petit homme que Rameau!

Of the above criticism we would observe that it is one that regularly makes its appearance at the springing up of every new art-tendency, but is none the less senseless on that account. For, what is called "naturalness" in music is simply the result of the habituation of the ear, and the reproach constantly made to the pioneer composer — that he purposely heaps up difficulties — merely betrays the laziness of the objectors, who are unwilling to take any pains to explore the new art-domain opened to them by the genius of the artist. Subsequently also, on the appearance of every new opera, RAMEAU was subjected to the same attacks, although after the production of his opera "Castor and Pollux" (1737) he was acknowledged, even by his opponents, to be the first dramatic composer of France. The prominent position he had acquired at the Grand Opera, for which he produced in the following years twenty-two additional larger works, he retained up to his death (1764), and the manner in which the French nation honored the memory of the master, both by a magnificent funeral and by the memorial ceremonies on the anniversary of his death, repeated year by year, testifies that she numbered him, even in his life-time, among the best of her children.

Not less considerable are the merits that RAMEAU acquired through his epoch-marking labors in the field of musical theory. Whilst his predecessors had contented themselves with laying down rules for the *connection of chords*, without exploring their *origin*, in his "Traité d'harmonie", published in 1722, he succeeds in establishing this origin. His system is based on the over-tones or harmonics of a fundamental tone, viz: the Octave, the Fifth in the second Octave (or Twelfth), and the Third in the third Octave (Seventeenth). By transposing the Fifth and the Third — the former an Octave, the latter two Octaves lower — he obtains the major Triad, called by him "accord parfait"; the *minor* Triad ("accord parfait mineur"), on the other hand, is composed of three tones having a common over-tone, as. A, c, e, to which e is respectively Twelfth, Seventeenth and Octave. By adding Thirds to the Triad RAMEAU obtains the Septimachord and the Nonachord;[*] but those chords in which the Fourth and the Sixth are characteristic tones he obtains by the so-called "inversion" of the Triad or the Septimachord. Besides this system, which forms the basis of harmonic theory up to the present time, the musical world owes to RAMEAU also the introduction of the *equal temperament*, *i. e.*, the division of the Octave into twelve half-steps of equal dimensions, and with it the removal of the impediments that instrumental music, as far as instruments with fixed tuning are

---

[*] I venture to suggest the substitution of these two terms, legitimately derived from the Latin, for the cumbrous corresponding ones, "Chord of the Seventh", "Chord of the Ninth". *Translator.*

concerned, had till then had to encounter in its free development. SEBASTIAN BACH had already in 1722 brought the equal temperament into use by means of his "Wohltemperirtes Clavier"; but after the appearance of RAMEAU's "Génération harmonique" (1737) that system of tuning was universally accepted by theoreticians also as fundamental postulate of modern music, and with it the reduction of the ancient *modes* to the *Ionian* and *Æolian* (our *major* and *minor**). These latter had, centuries before, obtained in the folk-song almost exclusive application; they could not but attain to universal sway after the introduction of the equal temperament, implying the use of all the twelve tones of the Octave as tonics of as many transpositions of the major and the minor scale, and with it the breaking down of the obstacles put in the way of modern composition by the ancient modes.

Owing to the eagerness with which RAMEAU had for many years long devoted himself almost exclusively to theoretical speculation, and afterwards also, over and above his labors for opera, was incessantly occupied in defending his achievements in the theoretical domain against attacks at home and abroad, his character could not well have been free from one-sidedness. If he cannot be charged also, as was his predecessor LULLI, with heartlessness, yet he cared, especially when engaged with theoretical problems, but little or nothing for the outside world. In consequence he did not lack personal enemies, one of whom, the philosopher DIDEROT, whom he had angered by his opposition to his Encyclopædia, could say of him in his book "Le neveu de RAMEAU": "He is a philosopher in his way, he thinks only of himself, and the rest of the world is to him not worth a pin's head. His wife and daughter may die when they like; if only the church-bells of the diocese that toll at their funeral sweetly re-echo the twelfth and seventeenth, he is perfectly satisfied."

A dangerous rivalry with the Paris Grand Opera was created in the year 1752 by the arrival of an Italian opera-troupe, which obtained permission to produce comic operas and had, especially with PERGOLESE's intermezzo "La serva padrona", uncommon success. Immediately after the arrival of the Italians musical Paris had split into two parties, which, under the name of *Bouffonites* and *Anti-Bouffonites* took sides with either the

* See *Note*, p. 19.

Italians or the national opera. Both factions defended with equal obstinacy the chosen stand-point, and as the battle grew hotter and hotter the Italian singers at the end of two years thought best to abandon the field. The stir they had raised was, however, not to be lost on dramatic music in France. "As in every domain of intellectual life", says GOETHE, in his translation of DIDEROT's "Le neveu de Rameau", "so too in that of grand opera people had begun to be impatient of the rigid shackles of tradition, and the Italian Bouffonites had shown the possibility of demolishing the old, hated frame-work and acquiring a fresh plane for new efforts.... All the arts were in the middle of the preceding century characterised by an extraordinary, almost incredible affectation, and divorced from all art-truthfulness and simplicity. Not only had the romantic fabric of the opera become more rigid and unyielding through tradition, tragedy also was played in farthingales, and a hollow, affected declamation recited her master-works. This went so far that the wonderful VOLTAIRE, in delivering his own pieces, fell into an expressionless, monotonous, psalm-singing bombast, and was persuaded that in this way the dignity of his pieces, which deserved a far better treatment, obtained just expression."

No wonder that at such a time the sagacious heads among the French in all spheres of intellectual life united in the endeavor to oppose to culture and art what they called *nature*. In painting, LEBRUN's pompous and ambiguous representations were supplanted by the pictures of rural and family life, the genre-scenes of a WATTEAU and a LIOTARD; the mathematically planned gardens and clipped trees of LOUIS the fourteenth's court-gardener, Le Nôtre, had to give way to parks in the English style: but dramatic music shows a predilection for the operetta, and develops it after the model of the Italian *opera buffa* into the *Opéra-Comique*. True, there had been something of this sort before the arrival of the Italians in France, but as it was exclusively devoted to the amusement of the masses, it could in no way fulfil higher artistic requirements. The first step towards the artistic elevation of this opera of the masses was the performance of the works left behind them by the Italians, first of all, of the "Serva padrona" in a French version; then appeared the poet VADÉ and the composer DAUVERGNE with an original work, the comic opera

"Les troqueurs". After the complete success of this attempt the most noted poets of France, foremost FAVART and MARMONTEL, joined the new movement, substituting for the antique materials exclusively made use of for grand opera, events of daily — especially of civil — life, as subject-matter of their dramatic poems. The most prominent of their musical collaborators were: the Neapolitan DUNI, whose "La laitière" made its way to Germany and helped to naturalize comic opera in that country also; then the Frenchmen PHILIDOR (celebrated, over and above, as chess-player), MONSIGNY, whose "Le déserteur" (1769) is to this day favorably received in France; finally GRÉTRY, who, though half foreigner (born at Liége in 1741), gave comic opera that perfection through which it is down to the present time the genuine representative of the national character of the French in the domain of dramatic music.

In close alliance with this transformation of art-taste in France is the tendency exhibited at the same time by the French philosophy. The so-called *philosophy of enlightenment* is essentially opposition to the current dogmas and existing state of things in church and state, and the establishment of a new theoretical and practical view of life on naturalistic principles. Of the representatives of this tendency we will here name only JEAN JACQUES ROUSSEAU, as having acquired great renown not only as philosopher but also as musician, in the domain of theory by his "Dictionnaire de la Musique", published in 1767, popularized in countless later editions and translations into foreign languages; in that of practice by the opera written and composed by him, first performed in 1752, "Le devin du village". Just as in ROUSSEAU's religious, political and pedagogic principles the yearning to escape the ill of a degenerate society by returning to an imaginary state of nature finds extravagant utterance, so he wages war with like bitterness against the then ruling standards of musical taste, and is of course seen, in the quarrel between the Bouffonites and Anti-Bouffonites, on the side of the former.

In his "Letter on French music" he unmercifully lashes the stiff formality of grand opera; and though in some points he goes too far, as, for instance, in his aversion to polyphonic music, which, following the lead of Caccini (see p. 61), he declares an offence against good taste, yet most of the views therein expressed merit unqualified approbation. Especially will his demands that the orchestra should never come to a stop in the opera, but, even when the singing ceases, should follow up the train of thought of the actor; moreover, that in passionate scenes the perfect cadence should absolutely be avoided;* finally, that the librettist, instead of aiming at the greatest possible clearness, should rather let the auditor occasionally have the satisfaction of partly reading the meaning of the words in the soul of the singer — these demands will strike the champions of the modern tendency of the musical drama as perfectly legitimate. In connection with the last-mentioned observation we hear him repeat the objection made to the French language a century before, that it is ill adapted to be used with music, not precisely because of the difficulty of pronunciation, or of the nasal sounds and mute syllables, etc., but on account of its strictly logical construction as opposed to freedom of transposing members of a sentence, of inversions, which in the Italian language sustain the attention up to the end of the sentence and at the same time the interest for the accompanying music.**

From this prejudice ROUSSEAU was freed only through that musician who brought the LULLI opera to the highest degree of perfection, again (strange to say) a foreigner, Chevalier CHRISTOPHER VON GLUCK (born in 1714 at Weidenwang, Bavaria, died at Vienna, in 1787).*** Through his powerful artist-personality GLUCK succeeded, after a comparatively unsuccessful career as opera-composer in Italy and Germany, in finding in Paris the suitable soil for his musico-dramatic reformatory efforts. Again, at his appear-

---

* "Ces cadences parfaites sont toujours la mort de l'expression", so we read in the work here referred to.

** "Si je voulois m'étendre sur cet article, je pourrois peut-être vous faire voir encore que les inversions de la langue italienne sont beaucoup plus favorables à la bonne mélodie que l'ordre didactique de la nôtre, et q'une phrase musicale se développe d'une manière plus agréable et plus intéressante, quand le sens du discours, longtemps suspendu se résout sur le verbe avec la cadence, que quand il se développe à mesure, et laisse affoiblir ou satisfaire ainsi par degrés le désir de l'esprit, tandis que celui de l'oreille augmente en raison contraire jusqu' à la fin de la phrase", etc.

*** GLUCK owed his title of "Chevalier" to the decoration, received from the Pope, of the Cross of the Golden Spur, a distinction afterwards conferred on MOZART also.

ance, the Parisian public were divided into two parties; this time, however, the friends of progress, among them ROUSSEAU, stood on the side of the French grand opera, while the adherents of the existing state of things placed their hope in Italian music. Still more fiercely than at the time of the Bouffonites and the Anti-bouffonites raged the battle between the Gluckites and their adversaries, who, after the Neapolitan composer PICCINI had been set up as rival of the German master, called themselves "Piccinites"; nor was it till after many years that the contest was decided, in consequence of the victory achieved by GLUCK's "Iphigenia in Tauris", in 1781, over the opera of the same name by PICCINI, on which occasion German music celebrated in the domain of opera its first triumph over Italian and French music.

From all that has been said of the character of the French grand opera it follows that it was by no means accidentally that France became the theatre of GLUCK's reformatory activity. For, just as little as it was his intention to follow, as musician, the taste of any nation whatever, so too he could not doubt that the tendency given to dramatic music by LULLI and RAMEAU, and only this tendency, could guarantee the realization of his own principles; that moreover, the characteristic inclination of the French opera public of that day (as also of the present time) to enjoy music reflectively rather than directly, would afford him the greatest possible freedom in practically carrying out his system. How conscious he was of his special mission as dramatic composer, and what fixed principles he followed in his work, he shows us in the preface to his opera "Alceste", a kind of artistic creed, which at the same time expresses the opinion of the many, who before and after GLUCK have combated and will yet combat the excessive prominence of the music in the opera. The most important sentences of this significant preface are the following*: "When I undertook to set the opera "Alceste" to music, I resolved to avoid all those abuses which had crept into Italian opera through the mistaken vanity of singers and the unwise compliance of composers, and which had rendered it wearisome and ridiculous, instead of being, as it once was, the grandest and most imposing

---

* I have transcribed these extracts as they are given in GROVE's Dictionary of Music and Musicians, Vol. I, Part V.   *Translator.*

stage of modern times. I endeavored to reduce music to its proper function, that of seconding poetry by enforcing the expression of the sentiment, and the interest of the situations, without interrupting the action, or weakening it by superfluous ornament. My idea was that the relation of music to poetry was much the same as that of harmonious coloring and well-disposed light and shade to an accurate drawing, which animates the figures without altering their outlines. I have therefore been very careful never to interrupt a singer in the heat of a dialogue in order to introduce a tedious ritornelle, nor to stop him in the middle of a piece either for the purpose of displaying the flexibility of his voice on some favorable vowel, or that the orchestra might give him time to take breath before a long-sustained note."

"Furthermore I have not thought it right to hurry through the second part of a song if the words happened to be the most important of the whole, in order to repeat the first part regularly four times over; or to finish the air where the sense does not end, in order to allow the singer to exhibit his power of varying the passage at pleasure. In fact, my object was to put an end to abuses against which good taste and good sense have long protested in vain."

"My idea was that the Overture ought to indicate the subject and prepare the spectators for the character of the piece they are about to see; that the instruments ought to be introduced in proportion to the degree of interest and passion in the words; and that it was necessary above all to avoid making too great a disparity between the Recitative and the Air of a dialogue, so as not to break the sense of a period or awkwardly interrupt the movement and animation of a scene. I also thought that my chief endeavor should be to attain a grand simplicity; and consequently I have avoided making a parade of difficulties at the cost of clearness; I have set no value on novelty, as such, unless it was naturally suggested by the situation and suited to the expression; in short, there was no rule which I did not consider myself bound to sacrifice for the sake of effect".

The practical carrying out of these maxims could of course find no applause either in Italy nor in the artist's native land, utterly dominated as it was by Italian opera. In Germany he had for opponents not only the whole body of musicians but also the most eminent critics, among them Professor FORKEL, of Göttingen, who employed all his esthetic sagacity in depreciating GLUCK's music, and was especially severe upon the composer's claiming for it the property of "noble simplicity". "What the Chevalier pleases to call 'noble simplicity' is in our opinion nothing but a miserable, empty and naked, or, to speak more properly, an *ignoble* simplicity, arising from lack of art and knowledge. It is like the stupid simplicity of the common people as against the noble simplicity shown in the manners and conversation of polished and meritorious persons; in the former case everything is coarse, deficient and faulty, but in the latter, perfectly correct, plain and elegant. In a word, the GLUCK species of noble simplicity resembles the style of our alehouse-virtuosi, which has in it simplicity enough, to be sure, but at the same time much that is disgusting."

For criticisms of this kind GLUCK was, indeed, up to a certain degree indemnified by the enthusiastic approbation bestowed upon him in literary circles: his very remark to the librettist of his "Iphigenia in Aulis", DU ROLLET: "Before I set to work I first of all try to forget that I am musician", should have sufficed to secure for him the sympathy of cultivated non-musicians. Nevertheless, the influence of these circles upon public opinion was, under the social and political circumstances of Germany at that time, too insignificant for GLUCK to expect from them an effective support of his efforts. It was otherwise in France, where just then in all departments of intellectual life the fashion was set by the representatives of literature, and where in this case the most eminent philosophers and poets had worked together to gain the victory for GLUCK's opera. Especially must the voice of a man of ROUSSEAU's authority have weighed much in GLUCK's favor, after the former had openly acknowledged that GLUCK's opera had entirely cured him of his former unbelief in the possibility of a French music-drama. And that this acknowledgement by no means concerned theoretical principles merely, that GLUCK's music fully satisfied the philosopher's intellect not only but also the craving of his heart and soul, is proved by the fact that ROUSSEAU, after having refrained for years from visiting the opera, from the time of the appearance of the "Orpheus" missed no representation of the work, as also by his answer to the reproach of want of melody made against GLUCK's music: "I find that melody streams out from all his pores".

The political disturbances that a few years after this second musical contest convulsed the French capital, were anything but favorable to the farther development of dramatic music in France. True, the theatres were, as a contemporary (CHERUBINI's wife) relates, crowded at night, after multitudinous guillotinings by daylight; moreover, the principal composers were constantly employed in glorifying the revolutionary proceedings by national hymns and other occasional works, yet the musical productions of that period have had no influence beyond the time of their origin, with one exception — the "*Marseillaise*", written and composed by ROUGET DE LISLE (produced for the first time under its original title: "Chant de guerre pour l'armée du Rhin", and scored by GOSSEC, on the 30th of September, 1792, at the Paris Grand Opera), which, as is well known, has retained its stimulating power from that day to this. Strange to say, however, to this period of wildest excitement belongs a musical event of thoroughly peaceful character and of the highest interest for music in general as for French opera in particular — the establishment of the Paris *Conservatory*. This institution, whose official name "Conservatoire de musique et de déclamation" expresses its aim as fosterer not only of music but also of dramatic acting, was designed, according to the plan of its founder, SARRETTE, primarily for the education of French military musicians, as up to that time Germans were the only ones to be had. But after the government had assumed the care of the school originally supported by SARRETTE out of his private means, its sphere of activity was enlarged; the first musicians of France* came together to labor in common, and as first fruit of their activity appeared a number of instruction-books for all branches of musical technics, the utility of most of which has been attested down to the present day. In other respects also the labors of those men were accompanied with the best success, so that in but few years after the opening of the institution the Germans were no longer needed. The German spirit, indeed, continued even thenceforward to influence French music, as is proved, e. g., by the works of MÉHUL, whose "Joseph in Egypt" (1807) makes no concessions to the national taste of

---

* Among them GOSSEC, MÉHUL, CHERUBINI, the last-named from 1821 to 1842 director of the Conservatory; he was followed by AUBER (died 1871), and the latter by AMBROISE THOMAS.

the French: farther, by those of CHERUBINI, who as opera-composer first made his mark in Vienna, and was acknowledged by the musicians there, including BEETHOVEN, as insurpassable master in this kind; lastly by those of SPONTINI, who, although the genuine musical representative of Napoleonic France, yet as musical dramatist closely follows GLUCK, and during the larger part of his artist-career labored in Germany, specifically in Berlin, where he had from 1820 to 1841 the position of general music-director. The French spirit, on the other hand, from henceforward finds its expression almost exclusively in comic opera, and here in its greatest purity in BOIELDIEU ("Caliph of Bagdad", 1800: "John of Paris", 1812), and AUBER ("The Mason", 1825).

To the many foreigners who, influenced by the national taste, became tributary to French grand opera, we must yet add MEYERBEER (born at Berlin, 1794, died at Paris, 1864). He might, by reason of his brilliant musical talent and his insight and experience in regard of dramatic effect, have been the man to promote French opera in every direction, had he not allowed the desire for outward effect to prevent him from rightly and conscientiously applying his gifts. In this endeavor he almost entirely loses sight of art-fitness and purity of style and is in the main satisfied with astonishing the public by constantly employing new stimulants. The applause which nevertheless his operas have met with in France and everywhere, accounts for the fact that the latest generation of composers for grand opera have in the main followed his example. On the other hand, it appears that the more ideal tendency of dramatic music so ardently pursued for the last decennium in Germany has found numerous followers among the French musicians of the present time. From them we may expect with certainty an enrichment and ennobling of French opera, provided that they avoid the rock on which so many of their countrymen have been shipwrecked: the giddy pursuit of quick artistic successes, the over-estimation of the *vox populi* at the expense of their musical conscience.

VIII.
GERMAN OPERA.

Opera in Germany — as the title of this chapter ought in strictness to read, seeing that a national opera, such as Italy and France had possessed as early as in the 17th century, could, during the period to be described, not, or at least only imperfectly, be developed among the Germans — opera in Germany took, like French opera, its start from the Italian, and it is a remarkable fact that the Fatherland anticipated all other countries in introducing the art-species newly discovered in Florence. It was the elector JOHN GEORGE I. of Saxony, that brought about the first opera-performance in Germany, the occasion being the marriage of his daughter to the landgrave of Hesse-Darmstadt, to which latter he wished to offer an art-enjoyment of a special nature. There was, to be sure, at that time no lack in Germany of theatrical representations of various kinds. For a century the sacred plays had, in consequence of the Reformation, been replaced by the so-called "Moralities", a kind of dramatic performance imported from France, having chiefly moral and theological aims, personifications of virtues and vices being mingled with the characters of bible-history. Alternately with these were played *Student-Comedies* in Latin and German, in which at the very beginning of the Renascence is seen the endeavor to bring about a regeneration of the drama after the classical pattern. Besides these, the *carnival plays* had sprung up from the midst of the people, which were arranged by guilds of citizens and artisans, and, after poets like HANS SACHS (end of the 16th century) and JACOB AYRER (beginning of the 17th century) had devoted their talents to them, aroused such interest that they were no longer restricted to the carnival season but were performed the whole year round.

Festivities of this kind, however, appeared to the elector insufficient for the entertainment of his guest, after the news of the revival of the antique music-drama had come to him from Italy. Accordingly he charged his court-music-director, HEINRICH SCHÜTZ (of whom we shall speak later), to order from Florence PERI's and RINUCCINI's maiden opera "Daphne", and the poet MARTIN OPITZ to turn the text into German. As, however, the German version would not suit PERI's music, SCHÜTZ was obliged to set it to original music, and now at last (April 13, 1627) the opera could be performed. As to the success of this performance we are left in uncertainty: SCHÜTZ's music, too, has not been preserved, which would be deplorable were we not justified in assuming that the composer closely imitated the Italian style, of which he was a fervent admirer. It was not possible that this first appearance of opera should have a permanent effect, for the reason that soon afterwards the disturbances of the Thirty Years' War rendered infeasible the promotion of the arts in general. As for SCHÜTZ, after the restoration of an orderly state of things he no longer composed for the theatre,* but devoted himself to sacred music exclusively, leaving opera to the Italians who came to Dresden in 1662, after the regular theatrical performances had been renewed upon the accession of JOHN GEORGE II. to the throne. To set up domestic against foreign art would have met with as little encouragement here as in the other capitals of Germany, since the political and material distress consequent upon the war seemed to have paralyzed for ever the intellectual elasticity of the people, and with the exclusive preference of the princes for everything foreign it was all the easier for Italian opera to attain absolute dominion.

One single city of Germany made at that time an exception — *Hamburg*, which on account of its geographical position had had less to suffer from the ravages of war, and by its commercial energy had for a long time attained to wealth, but at the same time so earnestly pursued the ideal aims of life that in this re-

---

* With the single exception of one work, the "Orpheus", composed after a second journey to Italy, performed Nov. 20, 1638, at Dresden, the music of which is also no longer extant.

spect, especially as nursery of music, it had during the second half of the 17th century the highest reputation throughout all Germany. How highly art and its representatives were esteemed here is shown by the fact (among others) that CHRISTOPH BERN-HARD, when he was called from Dresden to be town-precentor,* was ceremoniously received by the notables of the city, who rode in six coaches as far as Bergedorf — two miles distant — to meet him. Especially was there in Hamburg no lack at any time of excellent organists: among them must be specially mentioned JOHANN ADAM REINKEN, whose playing had such an attraction for SEBASTIAN BACH (among others) that the latter during his school-days repeatedly made his way on foot from Lüneburg to Hamburg to hear the master. Under these circumstances sacred music was necessarily the first to feel the influence of the progress made in Italy through the development of the dramatic element in music. Hamburg consequently became the place for solving the question, discussed everywhere in Germany, whether in church-music the simple, sombre ancient style, or a "subdued theatrical" style with strong emotions and touching expression, should be preferred. The Hamburg composers KEISER, MATTHE-SON, TELEMANN, advocated the latter style, and urged that "as the divine music best exhibited its excellency in opera, the most fashionable piece of poetry, so much the more reason was there for giving a like advantage to church-music, consecrated directly to God's glory". On the basis of these principles and by adapting the vocal forms of Italian opera to sacred texts were first produced the great church-cantatas, then the "Passion" in the form in which BACH afterwards brought it to perfection.

At first this dramatic church-music found universal applause. Even among the clergy there was no lack of earnest advocates of the new tendency, in fact some of their number had themselves given the impulse to the movement, as for instance ERD-MANN NEUMEISTER, who had for many years written texts of church-cantatas in operatic form. When, however, the poets began, by individual — for the most part anything but sublime — inspiration, to crowd the sacred text more and more out of the

---

* *Stadtcantor* in German, one who is appointed to have charge of the music in the churches of a town or city.   *Translator.*

Passion-poems, the orthodox clergy felt that they were called upon to protest energetically against the mixture of sacred and secular, and from the contradiction of opinions sprang a literary feud which lasted for years, and even extended far beyond the limits of Hamburg.

This short indication of the attempts originated at Hamburg towards the formation of a new church-style — the farther results of which will be discussed in the next section — may suffice to explain why precisely Hamburg could undertake to lead the way in the domain of opera also. Until 1678 the German song-plays performed here were mere imitations of the French operettas; but meanwhile the innovations in church-music had awakened the impulse to aim at higher things for the theatre also. Not only the artistic body and the most respected citizens, but also part of the clergy were altogether favorable to the plan of a national opera: the preacher at St. Catherine's church, ELMENHORST, not satisfied with publicly approving of it, coöperated personally in its accomplishment by writing opera-texts. In the year above mentioned, however, these wishes were to find their realization through the agency of the organist REINKEN, who had united with others in a theatrical undertaking in grand style, and on the 2d of January the first German opera-house was opened with the opera "Adam and Eve, or the created, fallen and redeemed man", text by RICHTER, music by music-director THEILE.

The interest aroused by this first attempt in all circles of the population of Hamburg must have excited hope for the prosperity of German opera. The German national feeling could here all the more readily put its stamp on the foreign product, in that, owing to the republican constitution of the city, every regard for court and aristocracy was dispensed with. If nevertheless the Hamburg opera could not be brought to a complete whole it was not for lack of able composers, but owing to the dissension between the poetic dilettanteisms of the experts and those of the people, for which there was no suitable mediator among the poets of that time. It was impossible for the people to take delight in the sacred and antique materials exclusively employed at that time, for which reason it was judged necessary to infuse into even the most serious situations a ludicrous element. At the same time no pains were spared to gratify the sense of sight, and accordingly the operas were got up as to externals with a carefulness strikingly contrasting with the slovenliness and hollowness of the poems. Not the least of the difficulties with which the Hamburg opera had to contend was the lack of efficient singers, especially females: the *castrati* had never been liked in Hamburg, and the daughters of semi-respectable families were deterred by the dominant prejudices against the theatre from devoting themselves to the stage. Accordingly one had to take, as DOMMER says (History of Music), what one could get: under the mask of Olympic gods and heroes were sheltered cobblers and tailors, runaway students and vagabonds of all sorts, and similarly the mistresses of the fish and vegetable markets figured along side of the priestesses of Venus vulgivaga as antique goddesses and queens.

A new life began for the Hamburg opera with the advent of music-director KUSSER (or COUSSER) from Pressburg (1693), who introduced, first, by means of his operas modelled after those of STEFFANI, a better style of writing and of singing, then also a stricter discipline among the actors, and through his energy combined with amiability accomplished all that under the circumstances was possible. His exertions as composer, and as director and teacher of the artists committed to his care were so successful that MATTHESON in his book "The perfect music-director" held him up as the ideal of one holding that office. But still more genial than KUSSER's were the labors of the Leipsic composer REINHARD KEISER, who settled in Hamburg in 1694, and in a short time became, through his fresh, vigorous talent, the hero of the day. KEISER's productivity was extraordinary: he wrote 120 operas, some of which were given even in Paris, though without special success, as they were inferior from the dramatic side to the French operas, and, as regards vocal effect, to the Italian. His music was well spoken of by his contemporaries, but as he had no higher aim than to please the public of his day, he became more and more estranged from the ideal and his talent steadily declined.

It is characteristic of the freshness inherent in the music-life of Hamburg that even a HANDEL was attracted by it and devoted his efforts for three years — 1703 to 1706 — to the theatre of that city. Notwithstanding all this, the Hamburg opera fell in a few decennaries from the height so quickly attained: external stimulants were more and more recklessly supplied, to make up for interior barrenness of style. Heaven and hell, battles and other spectacles were represented: horses, asses, camels and monkeys appeared more and more frequently on the stage; the fool and the merry-Andrew played their pranks, in the serious opera as in the farce, with ever increasing obtrusiveness. Even TELEMANN, famous far beyond the boundaries of Germany, who was called from Frankfort in 1721 to prop up the opera after MATTHESON and KEISER had already withdrawn from it, could not prevent its fall: in 1738 German opera is utterly discontinued, and the Italians, for a long time already supreme in the other capitals of Germany, now make their triumphal entry into Hamburg also.

After the failure of the Hamburgers to sustain a national opera, nothing is heard for some decennaries of farther attempts in this direction. About the middle of the century, however, German opera begins to stir itself, in connection with the upward flight of German poetry brought about by the poets of the so-called Prussian school of Frederick the Great's time — UZ, GLEIM, RAMLER, KLOPSTOCK, LESSING. In the domain of the musical drama this movement is manifested in a threefold way, and that, too, each time under foreign influence. GLUCK finds in LULLI's French opera the most suitable means of asserting the power of his German spirit as opposed to the Italian effeminacy; MOZART selects SCARLATTI's Italian opera as the starting-point of his own — interiorly likewise good — German art-endeavors: finally, the French comic opera, called into life at the same time by the help of the Italian *opera buffa*, suggests the idea of re-instating and ennobling the *German song-play.** These reformatory efforts had sprung, in Germany as in France, from the desire to return from an art estranged from everything natural to primitive simplicity and to an unaffected manner of feeling. Naturally, in this the song-play fell into the opposite faults of the grand opera: while the latter had lost the basis of reality under its feet, the former degenerated into coarse commonplace. But it made up for this by bringing into prominence two vivacious elements, jest and

---

* In the original German *Singspiel*, meaning a form of opera admitting spoken language, thus differing from *grand* opera. (*Translator.*)

drollery, which were calculated to atone for much that was defective, even though the means employed were not always of the most refined.

This time *Leipsic* is the city to hold out its hand to German opera in its bold attempt to dispute the field with the Italian. Here in 1765 the first song-play was performed, entitled "The Devil is loose, or, The transformed women", the libretto (from English material) by the poet WEISSE, the music by JOHANN ADAM HILLER, cantor at the St. Thomas church. The latter had, in his endeavor to raise the art-species to a higher plane of art, to contend with a twofold difficulty. In the first place, the theatre-director KOCH required of him that the music should throughout be so simple that each one of the audience could occasionally join in it; in the next place, the singers proved utterly incapable of accomplishing what HILLER required of them, seeing that now, as formerly in Hamburg, the best vocalists had been secured by the Italian opera. The Prussian music-director REICHARDT writes concerning this: "As often as there came an air by HILLER which was full of noble feeling and very expressive, I imagined to myself how he used to sing it to me at his piano, and then I had to listen to the bawling of this or that big-mouthed female singer and the night-watchman's voice of the lover". Notwithstanding all this HILLER's operas were universally liked and were spread over all Germany, especially "The Village barber" and "The Hunt", which latter was performed in Berlin in 1771 no less than forty times in the course of the year.

In Vienna German song-plays and operettas had already before this been performed by itinerant theatrical troupes, and as early as 1751 a JOSEPH HAYDN had tried his powers in this department. But his operetta "Der krumme Teufel" (a satire on the impresario AFFLIGIO), like MOZART's song-play "Bastien und Bastienne", performed in private in 1768, could not exercise any influence upon the farther development of that species, because both works, as youthful and occasional productions, could not lay claim to higher art-worth and general estimation. Not until the going into effect of the emperor JOSEPH II.'s German-national tendencies does operetta begin to lift up its head. From the time of his accession (1765) this monarch had patronized the German stage, as an indispensable aid to national culture, and in later years he came to the determination to suppress utterly Italian opera and the ballet, in order to substitute for them the "national song-play", as he called German opera. The artist whom JOSEPH II. after a long search found worthiest to begin the series of German opera-composers was IGNAZ UMLAUF, then a viola-player in the orchestra, whose "Bergknappen" ("The Miners"), after gaining the emperor's approval at the general rehearsal, was in 1778 for the first time produced in public. Then followed a series of song-plays, partly translated from the Italian or French, partly written by Viennese poets and composers. Among the latter was MOZART also, whose long-cherished plan to write a German opera could now at last be carried out. He found a suitable libretto in BRETZNER's "Entführung aus dem Serail" ("Il Seraglio"); at the beginning of 1782 the composition was finished, and on July 12th of the same year the work was performed for the first time, amid the enthusiastic applause of the Viennese public.

Strangely enough, MOZART, in spite of this brilliant success, and although the "Entführung" came much nearer to the ideal set up by the emperor JOSEPH than all the works of previous composers, nevertheless received no commission for farther works of this kind. The emperor himself seems to have not clearly recognized the significance of what he had called into being, for he criticized MOZART's music rather coolly. "Too beautiful for our ears and very many notes, dear MOZART", said he to the composer, to which the latter replied: "Just so many notes, your Majesty, as are necessary." Much more deeply interested in MOZART's opera was the venerable master GLUCK, at whose request it was once performed even out of the opera-season. GOETHE, who had by his operetta-librettos "Erwin und Elmire", and "Claudine von Villabella" evinced his interest in the development of the German song-play, and had set great hopes on a third poem, "Scherz, List und Rache", set to music by his friend CHRISTOPH KAYSER, wrote shortly after the appearance of the "Entführung": "Unfortunately our piece suffered from a vocal leanness, it mounted no higher than to a terzetto, and one would have given a great deal for a chorus. Hence all our efforts to keep within the simple and limited were thrown away when MOZART appeared. The "Entführung" struck down every thing, and on the stage nothing was said of our so carefully prepared piece". In fact the German operetta, which had been opposed by men like GLEIM and LESSING as hurtful to culture and destructive of taste, had gained under MOZART a place among the serious, noble art-species. The master who in his Italian operas "Don Giovanni" and "Figaro" has proved his ability to transplant himself into the character and modes of expression of a foreign nation, shows himself in the "Entführung" a thorough German.

Incomparably greater applause than MOZART received was won from his contemporaries by the operetta-composer CARL DITTER VON DITTERSDORF, because he adapted himself in his artistic productions to the degree of musical culture of his surroundings, instead of rising above them, as MOZART did. After having passed through a strict school of composition, as shown by his string-quartets, which in sterling worth closely approach those of HAYDN, DITTERSDORF afterwards found in comic opera and *opera buffa* the proper field for his activity. The melodic richness of his music and the genuineness of his formations, constantly drawn from life, procured for him at his very first appearance as opera-composer with the "Doctor und Apotheker" (1786), a popularity such as neither HAYDN nor MOZART at that time enjoyed. The opera just mentioned was given in Vienna twenty times in the same year, and two years later in London thirty-six times in succession, and his other operas, some thirty in number, obtained like good fortune. Besides DITTERSDORF are to be mentioned as Viennese composers of song-plays JOHANN SCHENCK, famous through his "Dorfbarbier", also as musical adviser of the youthful BEETHOVEN; WENZEL MÜLLER, composer of more than two hundred song-plays of a low-comic order, among which "Die Schwestern von Prag" held its place on the German stage long after his death; FERDINAND KAUER, whose "Donauweibchen" was for a half century the delight of the frequenters of the popular theatres, — and others. The partiality of the public for these works of a lighter kind may well have disquieted those who had destined a more ideal sphere of action for German opera. But it was soon to be seen that these composers also had jointly helped to refine the national musical taste; for, when MOZART came forward on September 30, 1791 (the year of his death), with a second German opera, the "Zauberflöte", he was incomparably better understood than with his "Entführung". It is through the

"Zauberflöte" that Mozart has opened to his nation the sanctuary of German art. While in the case of the "Entführung" the primary purpose was to lift up the German song-play to the level of the opera, here the main point was to find forms which would allow perfect freedom to dramatic characterization. How the master succeeded in this is seen in every measure of the score — excepting of course the two arias of the "Queen of night", which he wrote out of consideration for the "voluble throat" of his oldest sister-in-law, Frau Hofer, — and how his German nature, in spite of his long intercourse with Italian art, remains utterly unadulterated, is seen precisely in the "Zauberflöte" with convincing certainty, for instance, in the amiable carrying out of the popular figure of Papageno, and no less in the religious ceremonials of the opera that pertain to free-masonry.

Beethoven declared the "Zauberflöte" Mozart's greatest work, "for here he has shown himself as German master" — and by this utterance his own standing as *German* composer is sufficiently characterized. As such he too had to aim at the perfecting of German opera, yet it was not given him to surpass Mozart in this domain, because the chief problem of his age, the development of instrumental music, preëminently claimed his attention. As the study of dramatic and artistic singing was till the close of the previous century the indispensable basis of musical education, so had Beethoven also gone through this school, and indeed under the direction of Salieri, famous as teacher and as opera-composer (from Maria Theresa's time up to his death in 1825 court music-director in Vienna). Yet already in Beethoven's first opera, "Fidelio", which was also to be his only one, it was evident that he had by no means adequately utilized the vocal instructions of this master, and the complaints of "unsingableness" which were heard during the rehearsals of this opera were only too well-founded. For Beethoven, accustomed by the tractability of the instruments to indulge his flights of fancy without restraint, had neglected to take account of the conditions under which alone the human voice can attain to full effect. Just so little was he capable of doing justice to the scenic requirements, and as he moreover rejected with his peculiar obstinacy all suggestions of betterment, the reception of the "Fidelio" on its first appearance (Nov. 20, 1805) could not but be a cool one. The Viennese reporter of the journal "Der Freimüthige", edited by KOTZEBUE, wrote at that time: "A new opera by BEETHOVEN, 'Fidelio, or Conjugal Love', did not please. It was performed but a few times, and, after the first representation, to empty houses. The music also is really far below the expectations to which experts and amateurs thought they had a right. The melodies and the characterization, exquisite as much of it is, lack nevertheless that happy, striking, irresistible expression of passion that carries us away in MOZART's and CHERUBINI's works; the music has some charming passages, but it is far from being a perfect, or even a successful work".

In explanation of the slender applause bestowed on "Fidelio" on its first appearance, we must also take into account the unfavorable outward circumstances under which the work came before the public. A few days before, the court and the nobility of Vienna had been driven out of the city by the entrance of the French under NAPOLEON; the theatres remained at first quite empty, and the audience which by degrees gathered in them consisted exclusively of French soldiery. The "Fidelio" had somewhat better fortune when it was resumed in the following year, after the political situation had cleared up and moreover the composer had consented to a partial revision of his score. Then it again rested for some years, and it was not till 1814 that "Fidelio", newly retouched and represented for the third time, could be fully understood and become common property of the German people. Without venturing to place it beside, much less above, MOZART's masterworks in art-value, we must nevertheless regard it as a precious legacy of BEETHOVEN's genius. Here the master could of course not attest his whole power and originality, since the forms to which the opera was restricted at his time and which he did not as yet venture to demolish, offered insurmountable obstacles to his yearnings for artistic freedom. "While in the oratorio and especially in the symphony a noble, perfect form lay before the German master, the opera offered him an incoherent medley of small undeveloped forms, to which was attached a conventionalism incomprehensible to him and restrictive of all freedom of development. If we compare the broadly and richly developed forms of a BEETHOVEN symphony with the different pieces in his 'Fidelio', we at once perceive how the master here felt himself restrained and hindered, and could hardly ever attain to the proper unfolding of his power. For this reason, as if to launch forth at least for once in his entire fulness, he threw himself as it were with all the weight of desperation into the overture, projecting in it a composition of previously unknown breadth and significance. He withdrew in ill humor from this sole attempt at an opera, yet without giving up the wish to find a poem that would enable him to display his musical power. The Ideal it was, that was constantly before his mind."*

The prevailing state of operatic affairs at BEETHOVEN's time, on the one hand, and on the other his introverted, altogether subjective artist-nature explain why the "Fidelio" remained a solitary performance, a performance indeed in a high degree honorable to its author, yet not calculated to insure him a place among the corypheuses of German opera. He has, however, indirectly rendered to opera a highly important service, as it was he that gave the instruments a capability of expression unexcelled even to this day, to that extent that in the orchestra was found a tone-language for revealing the most secret emotions of the soul. With the aid of the Beethovenian orchestra the composers of the *romantic school* who succeeded BEETHOVEN ventured to undertake to guide German opera into new pathways, and under the fructifying influence of his genius it could become possible that a national music-drama, such as had long been possessed by Italy and France, should be brought to perfect maturity in Germany also.

---

* RICHARD WAGNER's "Zukunftsmusik". Collected Works, Vol. VII.

# IX.

THE ORATORIO.

The traces of the sacred music-drama, which, divested of external accessories, action, costume and decorations, has attained under the name "Oratorio" so great importance in the music-life of our day, can be followed up into a far more remote antiquity than those of the secular. Not only is the Greek tragedy to be classed, as a religious ceremony, in this category; the celebration also of the mysteries by the Egyptian priests, as described by HERODOTUS, in which were represented, undoubtedly with musical accompaniment, the sufferings of the god Osiris, may rank as a kind of passion-play, and similarly, among the Hebrews the rich temple-worship at King David's time, his dancing before the ark, and the antiphonal singing of the psalms, point to a musico-dramatic form of divine worship. The Christian church in early times united a dramatic element with its ceremonial, from the conviction that sensuous perception operated more powerfully on the minds of the new converts than mere doctrine. The gospel was at first acted out, or, as it was said afterwards, impersonated, whereby the whole action acquired a dramatic appearance: one priest recited the words of Jesus, another those of the evangelist; the multitude, the disciples and the Sanhedrim were represented by the choir of singers. As, however, the singing was in no wise distinguishable from that prescribed for the divine service, the difference between these representations and the usual ritual was scarcely noticeable.

A more marked prominence of the dramatic as also of the musical element is seen in the representations of the Passion that were usual, under the name "Planctus Mariæ" ("The Sorrows of

Mary"), during the 13th and 14th centuries. Here the metre of the poems proves that they were sung — not to a church-chant, but — to a melody of master-song, of a character about midway between the lightness of the folk-song and the gravity of the plain-chant. The religious drama made still farther advances in this direction, after the clergy, in order to turn the public favor from the very low secular plays to something higher, had brought forward the laity also to participate in it. In consequence of this societies were formed from among them for the purpose of getting up representations of this kind, — as for instance, in 1389 at Paris, the *Confrérie de la Passion*, to whom the king granted a theatre, called "la Trinité", for their own special use. In time, however, the coöperation of the laity, to whom the strolling musicians also united themselves, gave the sacred plays a secular, burlesque, even immoral stamp, and the music, which in the low-comic episodes connected with sacred history took the place of the *accentus ecclesiasticus*,* was, in order to agree with the situation, not permitted to rise above the folk-songs that were most popular as bordering on the street-songs, as for instance when JUDAS is haggling about the thirty pieces of silver, or when the ointment-vender is offering his wares to the women hastening to the Saviour's tomb, cracking the while all kinds of coarse jokes.

Still greater was the disorder connected with the so-called "Ass's festivals" and "Fools' festivals", celebrated up to the end of the Middle Age in some countries, chiefly in France. In the former festival, which was celebrated in memory of the flight of the holy family into Egypt, an ass covered with a monk's cowl was led through the streets into the church, the priest at the altar intoned the so-called ass's chant, and for a refrain imitated the ass's braying, whereupon the congregation dancing round the animal, responded antiphonally. The "Fools' festival", or "All Fools' day", was kept at the winter-solstice, in remembrance of the ancient Roman Saturnalia with their temporary emancipation of slaves; a fool-bishop was chosen to celebrate mass, while the rest of the clergy and the people, disguised as wild beasts — a

---

* The manner, half-way between singing and declamation, of intoning the prayers, epistles and gospels, lessons, etc. in the church-service.

reminiscence of the combats of beasts in the Roman circus — dealt blows right and left in the church and committed the grossest excesses. Just so little as all these spectacles can the *representations of Death in processions*, which sprang up at the same time, lay claim to artistic significance. These descend from an old traditional play on the feast of the seven Maccabean brothers — whence also the name "Chorea Maccabeorum" (Dance of the Maccabees), afterwards in France "danse macabre", — and enjoyed great popularity, as is attested by the manifold pictorial representations of the "Dance of Death" by the painters of the Middle Age.

For lack of the necessary means the popular drama was unable to expand, either towards the sacred or the secular side, into a higher art-species; it sank deeper and deeper, until in the 17th century it utterly disappeared. The last trace of it may be found in the *Passion-play* which is still performed every ten years at *Oberammergau* in Bavaria, and which in view of the fervor and the artistic tact of the coöperators, as also of the part taken in it by the thousands of spectators, is more than merely historically interesting. As for the ecclesiastical representations of sacred history, on the other hand, that had continued to exist side by side with the passion-plays of the laity, they had remained, over against the grotesque excrescences of the latter, true to their liturgical character, and were able, especially after the revival of church-song through the Reformation, to attain enhanced musical importance. At first it was of course impossible to break with the old music-forms; during the entire 16th century the evangelist continued to recite the history of the Saviour's passion in the *accentus ecclesiasticus*, the words of Christ were sung in four-part harmony, as though to divert the attention from his real personality and allow only the universal validity of his words to be emphasized. Even HEINRICH SCHÜTZ with whom as expert and friend of the dramatic music that sprang up in Italy at the beginning of the 17th century we became acquainted in the preceding section, could not find exactly new forms for the musical celebration of Easter, but could put a new spirit in the old ones, as a nearer view of his labors will show, after we shall have first taken a survey of Italy's efforts in this domain.

Italy, the fatherland of ecclesiastical and of dramatic music, is the birthplace, as of the opera, so also of the Oratorio. As early as in the course of the 16th century it had been customary in the monasteries there to establish in Lent public devotional exercises, to compensate the people for the theatrical plays forbidden during the penitential season. An additional attractiveness was given to these meetings — called, after the prayer-hall (oratory) in which they were held, *Congregazioni del oratorio* — when the Roman priest FILIPPO NERI came upon the idea of joining to his explanations of scripture sacred choral singing appropriate to them and calculated to illustrate them. At first ANIMUCCIA, predecessor of PALESTRINA as music-director at St. Peter's, conducted the musical part of the service and also composed for it a kind of four-voiced hymns under the name *Laudi spirituali*, in which occasionally one voice, or two voices, sustaining a colloquy, would break off from the four-part setting. After ANIMUCCIA's, death PALESTRINA took his place as both papal music-director and musical assistant of NERI; under his direction the colloquial form of these pieces was more strongly marked, they were grouped in scenes, and in this form were called *Azione sacra* (sacred action) or simply *Oratorio*, the name of the place of performance being transferred to the thing itself. — By the side of these two masters stands the Spaniard VITTORIA (from Avila near Madrid, 1575 music-director at St. Apollinaris' church, Rome), who, with many of his countrymen, at their head MORALES OF SEVILLE, who had in the first half of the century entered the papal choir, found in Rome the sphere of artistic activity which his own country was unable to offer him. The serious, deeply religious, somewhat mystic character peculiar to the works of these composers educated after Netherlandic patterns yet with the feelings of genuine Spaniards, is seen in VITTORIA, especially in his highly effective four-voiced *choruses of the people* (turbæ) in the Passion according to St. Matthew's gospel and that according to St. John's. These choruses, though mere ceremonial pieces for the ecclesiastical ritual and accordingly free from any dramatic intention, may nevertheless be considered as preparatory labors for the later oratorio-chorus.

It was about this time that the musical reform-movement begun at Florence gave artistic taste that entirely changed tendency from which, as its direct aim, the modern opera could come into existence, and it was natural enough that the church also, tired of worn-out formalism, was anxious to adopt the new kinds of style that had been gained for secular music. This was brought about first by EMILIO DEL CAVALIERE, until 1595 intendant of music to the ducal court of Florence, who had taken part in the initial attempts at reviving the ancient Greek music-drama, yet had not then found anything suitable to the purpose. If in consequence he had to forego the fame of being named among the founders of modern opera, he secured, in compensation, an honorable place in the history of the Oratorio. For, with the appearance of his sacred allegorical music-drama *La rappresentazione di anima e di corpo** (first performed in the year 1600 on a stage in the oratory of the monastery of Santa Maria in Vallicella at Rome), the two principal species of vocal and instrumental music connected with an action begin to develop themselves in their peculiar manner. The problem of the *opera* is from this time forth to unite music and poetry with an action visibly represented on the stage: the *oratorio*, on the other hand, aims at the adjustment of ecclesiastical and secular art on the territory of biblical history, and if it likewise at first admits visible action, yet the latter retires more and more into the background, until from HANDEL's time onward) the action is represented only in music.

A coöperator with CAVALIERE in the introduction of the dramatic style into church-music was LUDOVICO VIADANA (died after 1644 as music-director at Mantua), who by his *Concerti da chiesa*, pieces for one or more voices with an organ-bass, was the first to naturalize in the church the monody newly invented by CACCINI. Specially worthy of note in these "concerts" is the appearance of an independent obligatory instrumental bass, the *basso continuo*, so-called because, unlike the vocal bass, it makes no occasional pauses but gives the harmony a solid foundation throughout the whole piece. For this reason it was called also *bassus generalis*,** whence arose later the error of ascribing to VIADANA the inven-

---

* The name "rappresentazione" was, like "storia", "esempio", "misterio", a common designation of the Italian sacred drama. From time immemorial songs were mingled with these representations, mostly final choruses after the acts.

** The English equivalent of this would be the old-fashioned expression

tion of what is now called *figured bass*, *i. e.*, a bass with certain figures and signatures indicating the tones necessary to the completion of the harmony. This latter kind of bass was in use before his time, and occurs, *e. g.*, in PERI's opera "Euridice", which appeared two years earlier than the "*concerti da chiesa*". — But the most important part in the development of the oratorio as an independent art-species was taken by GIACOMO CARISSIMI (from 1528 onward music-director at St. Apollinaris' church at Rome), in that he moulded the till then simply song-like *cantata* into a kind of dramatic scene with recitative, airs and choruses, in which form it bore the name of *chamber-cantata*. Besides numerous works of this kind, which already is closely related to the later oratorio, CARISSIMI wrote also a series of actual oratorios, among them "Jephtha", "The Judgment of Solomon", and "Jonah", which are full of animated dramatic expression and especially rich in effective dramatic choruses and frequently recall HANDEL, on whose oratorios they exercised an influence similar to that which was exercised on his *operas* by those of ALESSANDRO SCARLATTI.

After CARISSIMI's death the sacred music-drama in Italy was utterly supplanted by the chamber-cantata, and at its re-appearance a century later it was seen to be thoroughly secularized by the spirit and the style of the opera. In the domain of *church-music proper* we meet, to be sure, even in the 18th century a number of Italian composers in whose works the traditions of their great predecessors still exert a powerful influence. Among these are the Venetians LOTTI (died in 1740 as music-director of St. Mark's), famous through his eight-voiced "Crucifixus"; CALDARA* (died at Vienna in 1736), whose sixteen-voiced "Crucifixus" is in art-worth not inferior to that of LOTTI; BENEDETTO MARCELLO, a Venetian nobleman and amateur, who, though excelled in talent by the two just mentioned, was able nevertheless by industry, versatility and intellectual activity to gain and maintain a brilliant position in the musical world. His chief work, the setting of *fifty Psalms of David* in an Italian version, procured him great fame among his contemporaries even outside of his native country. J. A. HILLER, in his "Wöchentlichen Nachrichten" (Leipsic, 1769) calls him a

---

"thorough-bass", *e. i.*, bass *throughout* ("thorough" here having its original meaning).   *Translator.*

* See p. 70.

man "who could unite the entire seriousness of the old music with the graces and the beauties of the new... In his Psalms he is so free and remote from all that is low or common, that an intelligent hearer is kept by an infinite variety of new and beautiful modulations in continual delight", etc. A peculiarity of this work of MARCELLO is his aim at antique simplicity, which he sought to attain by the use, among other things, of Hebrew ritual music, communicated to him by Spanish and German Jews. But granting that he was right in his opinion that these melodies came directly from the ancient Hebrew temple-song, still he only half accomplished his artistic purpose by his treatment of them. because in him (as VON DOMMER observes) the admirer and imitator of antiquity and the cavalier of the 18th century come in conflict. His antiquising* remains on the outside and attains to no intellectual blossom; the pretended antique simplicity forms a contrast to the language of modern subjective feeling and passion that MARCELLO's striving — under evident influence of the opera — after flexible, flowing song is by no means calculated to mitigate.

With incomparably greater care than in Italy were the Oratorio and the Passion fostered in Germany, where the most fearful of wars had annihilated material prosperity, indeed, yet not the ideal intellectual tendency. The very activity of the last great Netherlander ORLANDUS LASSUS, or ROLAND DE LATTRE, as music-director in Munich (where he died in 1595), among whose numerous master-works the seven *Penitential Psalms*, attesting deep, thoroughly German feeling, have a prominent place, points to Germany as the soil best adapted for the growth of ecclesiastical music. Immediately after him appear in HANS LEO HASLER (died in 1612) and JOHANNES ECCARD (died 1611) two artists who, though educated in foreign schools (the former in that of GABRIELI at Venice, the latter in that of ORLANDUS LASSUS), yet may be regarded as representatives of an independent German tone-art, and of whom the latter in particular, through his "Prussian festival songs for the whole year" — an intermediate species between motet and song, yet with more of the character of the latter — essentially enriched the protestant church-music. HEINRICH SCHÜTZ

---

* "Antiquise", to imitate the antique. *Translator.*

also (born in 1585, died in 1672 as music-director at Dresden), as pupil of GABRIELI utilized the inspiration received from Italy only for making his German depth and solidity avail to its whole extent, when, after his solitary attempt in the domain of the opera (see p. 93), he had turned his whole attention to church-music. The oratorio is indebted to him for a considerable advance, notwithstanding he wrote no work of that class in the modern sense; for his "Resurrection", and "Seven Words" belong in character rather to the species of Passion-music.

In the first of these works, printed in 1623 at Dresden, we still see a decided adherence to the old forms; the words of the title: "The Resurrection of our Lord Jesus Christ, as described to us by the four evangelists", set to music for six voices, serve as introduction; the words of the acting persons are likewise polyphonic, according to custom; the evangelist recites throughout according to the *accentus ecclesiasticus*, which is only occasionally interrupted by characteristic tone-progressions. A remarkable turn, on the other hand, in SCHÜTZ's career of artistic development is seen in his "Seven Words", published in 1645, in which the *recitativo arioso* has entirely supplanted the *accentus ecclesiasticus* and the monologues are invariably set for one voice. It is remarkable moreover that here the words of Jesus are not accompanied (as are those of the other personages) by the organ, but by stringed instruments, which, played in a high register, surround the voice as it were with a halo, a kind of accompaniment which, as is well known, has been applied in BACH's Matthew-Passion as also in later compositions of the same kind. Worthy of notice, moreover, is also the peculiar grouping of the material, already foreshadowing the future formation of the *Passion-text*: on the one hand the gospel history itself, clad, as action, in dramatic form, on the other hand the christian church, framing the proceedings with its feelings and reflexions in a broadly executed five-voiced introductory and final chorus. The peculiarly characteristic element of the Oratorio, the dramatically animated chorus, is not found either in the "Resurrection" nor in the "Seven Words", but occurs in SCHÜTZ's last work, the *"Four Passions according to the four Evangelists"* (1666), in which the dramatic feature operates the more powerfully in the choruses of the people for the reason that the aged master has, in regard of the shaping of the whole, returned to the older forms, the *accentus ecclesiasticus*, the polyphonic treatment of the monologue, etc. In those choruses, however, that ask, now timidly, "Lord, is it I?" now angrily, "Lord, shall we smite with the sword?" now cry in mockery, "Hail! King of the Jews", we see everywhere the effort not merely to accommodate the sense of the words to the sentiment but to represent it as action, and in this sense SCHÜTZ has more decidedly than CARISSIMI prepared the way for the HANDEL oratorio.

A long time had to elapse after SCHÜTZ's death before the discovery of forms for the Oratorio and the Passion by whose aid HANDEL and BACH could bring these art-species to the highest perfection. As regards the "Passion", we would cite, as farther noteworthy moments in its course of development: first, the appearance of a Passion-work by the Prussian music-director SEBASTIANI (1672), in which the protestant choral is interwoven into the musical representation of the passion at appropriate places conditionated by the sacred text. Next, the endeavors of the Hamburg librettists (see the preceding section) to reconcile the inclinations of the musical public with the demands of the orthodox clergy. To meet the opposition of the latter to the libretti then in favor, which were in form operatic and utterly unlike the old passion-forms, the licentiate BROCKES produced at the beginning of the 18th century a passion-text that was, to be sure, designed like the previous ones, yet in skilful grouping and dramatic fervor so far surpassed them that it was admired by contemporaries as a master-work and was set to music by the most eminent composers of Hamburg, viz: KEISER, MATTHESON and TELEMANN, and even by HANDEL (1716).

For the development of the "Passion" as art-species the text of BROCKES is of importance, because in it we find for the first time the three chief groups that afterwards appear in the BACH Passion: with the scenes out of the gospel history of CHRIST's sufferings are confronted the reflections and pathetic utterances of two allegorical personages, the "daughter of Sion" and the "believing soul", representing an assembly (the so-called "invisible church") accompanying in thought and explaining the actions and sufferings of CHRIST on earth: finally the protestant church and congregation also is represented by chorals, which, as with

Sebastiani, are at appropriate places connected by manifold allusions with the action.

Georg Friedrich Händel and Johann Sebastian Bach are the two artists whose memory should be doubly precious for the reason that their aim was directed at the realization of the highest art-ideals at a time when the older civilized nations — Italians and Frenchmen — applied themselves, at the cost of artistic seriousness, more and more to the cultivation of external effectiveness. We like therefore to mention especially their names in connexion, although they are seen to be, in their artistic nature as in their life-experiences, as different one from the other as possible. Both born in Thuringia and in the same year (Handel on Feb. 23d at Halle, Bach on the 21st of March at Eisenach), they develop themselves each in a particular direction, almost the opposite of the other. Bach was impelled by his nature to plunge into the depths of religious feeling, to penetrate into the innermost mysteries of religion, and this in conjunction with Pietism, the new theory of church-life introduced by Spener in 1675, according to which, in opposition to orthodoxy, not the words of Scripture or the sermon, but the personal interior enlightenment helps us to acquire divine knowledge.* He is, accordingly, before everything else lyric (see p. 11), in his whole manner of construction and of feeling subjective, almost romantic, hence, too, more at home in instrumental than in vocal music. Handel, on the other hand, finds his *point d'appui* in the outer world; the drama is

---

* Philipp Spitta, in his monograph "Ueber Sebastian Bach" (Leipsic, 1879), advocates the contrary opinion in regard of Bach, and substantiates it by showing that the general tendency of Pietism was inimical to art, moreover, by pointing to the fact that Bach, as organist at Nordhausen (1707), was, in the dispute of the theologians of that place, Eilmar and Frohne, on the side of the former, representing orthodoxy. Now, in this case no importance is to be attached to Bach's action, since he could, as artist and youth of twenty-two years, hardly have been influenced by any other than personal considerations. But that he should, with his marked idealistic and subjective nature, in riper years decide in favor of Pietism, follows from the very essence of this system, as it was not only far removed from Puritanical narrowness but in the main aspired to a warmer, more spiritual and freer appropriation of holy things, and precisely then concentrated in itself all of idealism and higher thought and feeling that was still alive in the German nation.

the art-species most nearly corresponding to his nature, consequently his art-conception is an objective, and in opposition to BACH's modern one, an antique one. As history is the domain in which by preference he moves, so too it is bible history in which his religious convictions take root: but as regards application of tone-material he is first of all vocal composer. BACH's existence flowed quietly as to externals, he never left his native country and was seldom absent from Leipsic, where he labored as cantor at the St. Thomas' school from 1723 until his death, and a journey to Dresden or to Berlin was to him an event. His choir and the organ of St. Thomas' church became his home, and while HANDEL extends under the influence of three nations the borders of his nationality, BACH, even if he does occasionally follow in his instrumental compositions French or Italian models, remains within the narrowest limits of national feeling. Thus the two heroes of German music also represent the double nature of the German people, viz: the devotion to what is foreign and the exclusiveness against it. But that neither the one nor the other was for a moment untrue to his German nature, is seen both in the character of their works and in the restless exertion and the never-flagging love of work which, even in their latest years after both had become blind) up to their death — BACH died 1750, HANDEL 1759 — never forsook them.

Influential as BACH's creative activity was in the most diverse departments of music, particularly upon the development of organ-playing and pianoforte-playing, yet it reaches its climax in the *"Passion"*. True, he did not create new forms for this art-species, nor did he attempt to find them; his merit is that he brought the traditional forms to the last possible perfection and filled them with matter corresponding to his musical giant-spirit. According to FORKEL* he wrote five "Passion" settings, of which however but two — those according to the Gospels of St. John and St. Matthew — were made public. The *St. John Passion*, the time of whose origin is unknown, exhibits in its forms the older pattern and in it we miss generally the dramatic impressiveness that so brilliantly stands out in BACH's later works. It is in the

---

* J. N. FORKEL, "Of JOHANN SEBASTIAN BACH's life, art and art-works". Leipsic, 1802.

St. Matthew Passion, first performed in 1729, that he appears to have at last fully recognized the greatness of his mission. Here is displayed his entire artistic ability: the skilful treatment of the protestant choral, the unlimited mastery of the fugue style, in which point even HANDEL has not equalled him, finally his knowledge of the orchestral instruments, which he frequently uses, according to their individual quality, by themselves alone, as *obligato* accompanists of a solo voice. The St. Matthew Passion is of art-historical importance in regard also of the text, inasmuch as BACH, while he had in the St. John Passion made use of parts of BROCKE's poem, here restored the text of the passion-history literally according to the gospel, hence too the accompanying reflections of the christian congregation and of the invisible church were introduced in greater moderation than before.

If now we confront with the Passion, so highly perfected by BACH, the Oratorio as art-species, the comparison must still turn out in favor of the latter, because in the former we find two — strictly speaking — reciprocally exclusive properties externally united, viz: the churchly in its purity and freedom from passion, and the dramatic with its powerful expression of the emotions, while in the oratorio the churchly and the secular dramatic elements are blended as a unit into a new species of art and style. This unity of style and form, which for the reason just given cannot exist in the Passion, the oratorio owes to HANDEL's activity in England, where he devoted himself to it exclusively and with his whole power, after having thoroughly gone through the school of opera in Hamburg, Italy, as music-director in Hanover and finally in London. It is highly creditable to England from a musical point of view to have brought to maturity on her soil one of the noblest and most important species of composition: for though her own children lacked the power necessary for this, yet the success of such an art-exploit presupposes a considerable sum of artistic labor and artistic feeling, of whose existence, moreover, the earlier music-history of England gives ample evidence.

The prominent musical position of England in the Middle Age already sufficiently shows that not lack of musical talent but outward circumstances are to be held responsible for the lack of independence of English music during the last two centuries. At that time England appears to be, as regards the cultivation of music, especially of organ-playing, by no means behind the other nations of the West; and the lively part that she afterwards took in the development of counterpoint is mentioned by the famous Netherlandic theorist TINCTORIS (about 1476 chief music-director to FERDINAND I. at Naples, author of the oldest musical lexicon, which appeared about the same time under the title "Terminorum musicæ diffinitorium"). This author goes so far as to maintain "that the fount and origin of this new art is to be found in England, where DUNSTABLE died about 1450) is conspicuous as its head". We will not attempt to test the correctness of this assertion, seeing that the artistic legacy of the above-named contrapuntist is at this day as good as unknown. Yet the fact speaks in its favor that the English singers and composers during the palmy days of Netherlandic counterpoint were everywhere and even in the home of the latter held in favor and sought for. But English music attained to the zenith of its development during the reign of QUEEN ELIZABETH, after the renascence-movement, originated in Italy, had given to the intellectual life of the island-kingdom also that impulse which was able to bring forth in the domain of poetry a SHAKESPEARE (1564—1616). At the same time with him appear as representatives of the sister-art a number of highly gifted composers and virtuosos, who must have been all the more impelled to activity as the queen herself gave the example, and showed her appreciation of music not only as expert performer on the virginal but also as protectress of church-music against the fanatical attacks of the Puritans. After her example the cultivation of solid music became so general that it was regarded as a sign of defective education if one should — for example — be unable to join, in an assembly, in the improvised execution of a piece of polyphonic vocal music. To judge from a passage from SHAKESPEARE's "Twelfth night", the partiality to contrapuntal singing seems to have been carried even to excess. "But shall we make the welkin dance indeed? Shall we rouse the night-owl in a catch, that will draw three souls out of one weaver?" asks Sir TOBY BELCH. And Sir ANDREW AGUE-CHEEK answers: "An you love me, let's do it: I am dog at a catch"! Nevertheless the possible abuses cannot in any wise dim the splendor of this golden age of English music, nor the fame of its chief representatives WILLIAM BYRD (from 1585 organist to the queen, in his time regarded as the English PALESTRINA, his pupil THOMAS MORLEY (editor of a valuable collection of madrigals, including many of his own composition, published in 1601 under the title "The triumphs of Oriana"), ORLANDO GIBBONS (noted organist, editor of the first music for the virginal printed in England), and the much-praised lute-virtuoso JOHN DOWLAND, of whose playing SHAKESPEARE says, in his "Passionate Pilgrim", "DOWLAND .... whose heavenly touch upon the lute doth ravish human sense".

In the farther course of the 17th century the progress of England's intellectual development was interrupted by the wars from which at the end a new form of government resulted. But after the restoration of internal order the nation was so busied with the care of material interests, and, after the destruction (in 1588) of the invincible Spanish Armada had laid the foundation of naval supremacy, with the strengthening of its position as a Power, that the ideal pursuits retired into the background and, as for music, the field was most willingly abandoned to foreign talent. The hospitable reception of CAMBERT in London (see p. 77, 79, as of the Italians who appeared before him, is characteristic of the eclectic tendency that musical England then inaugurated and has ever since followed. Even the most gifted of all English composers, the genial HENRY PURCELL, was unable to inspire anew confidence in the production of national music, and neither his numerous profound and magnificent church-compositions — among which the *Anthems* are specially noticeable —, nor his dramatic compositions, which are thirty-nine in number and as genuine home-products were well calculated to form the basis of a national English opera, were able in those unfavorable times to produce any lasting effect. "At such a time", says CHRYSANDER HANDEL, vol. I "a rigid disciplinarian is needed". — but such was PURCELL as little as MOZART was. For, earnestly as they pursued art, they took life just as easily and died early. But what PURCELL points to and desires is accomplished in HANDEL's life, and by the musical healthfulness of all his works and their unity of structure, as also by the versatility of his genius, he is that fore-runner of HANDEL that most directly leads to him.

A quarter of a century after PURCELL's early death, begin, with HANDEL's arrival in London, which from 1720 till his death was the scene of his labors, the golden days of the latter master, dating in fact from his engagement at the Italian opera at the Haymarket Theatre. The subversion of social relationships that had taken place in England at the beginning of the century had made it possible for opera to withdraw at this very time from the circles of the court and the nobility, and to look for support to the public, which had meanwhile artistically ripened. Under these circumstances HANDEL found during the twenty years of his theatre-life the best opportunity for learning to keep in view the art-necessities of the general public. But he had, on the other hand, also much to suffer from the disadvantages that the changed state of things brought with it for the artist-world. Aristocratic society, finding itself deprived of the sole direction in musical affairs, began to withdraw from the artists the material assistance formerly so generously bestowed, and HANDEL was not the man to make concessions in the matter of musical taste in order to turn the sentiments of the former art-patrons to his own advantage. Besides this, his duties as opera-director were rendered burdensome by the constantly increasing rivalry, especially after a second Italian opera-troupe, engaged by his enemies and directed by the Neapolitan PORPORA, had forced him to change the Haymarket for the Covent-garden theatre; none the less, too, by the petty jealousies of the male and female singers under his direction (see p. 71); so that in the year 1740, after the performance of his thirty-first opera "Deidamia", he gave up the theatre for good, after having lost through his last venture the whole of his painfully acquired fortune.

Meanwhile, however, his first oratorio "Esther" had in 1732 already been performed and received with hearty applause by that part of the London amateurs represented by the Academy of ancient music, who saw in HANDEL's work a realization of their plans for reviving the antique tragedy in the territory of biblical history. At that time opinions were divided, whether the oratorio should be given with acting or should entirely dispense with visible dramatic accessories. The bishop of London, Dr. GIBSON, decided in favor of the latter — to the no small advantage of HANDEL as musician, for now he could enjoy incomparably greater freedom in his creative work than under the constraint invariably suffered by the composer from the conditions of scenic representation. It is self-evident that dramatic music, when no longer supported by visible representation, is all the more required to give to all its forms the highest possible plasticity, sharpness and clearness, in order that the whole art-work may gain for our imagination and our feeling the semblance of perfect life and immediate presence, so that the absence of visible representation no longer impresses us as a defect. This applies both to the solo vocal parts and in a special manner to the choruses: indeed, the chorus, this weighty form for expressing popular and humanitarian ideas and feelings, may justly be considered as the centre of gravity of the HANDEL oratorio. "In it lies, just as in the chorus of the Greek tragedy, the sum of the moral and religious ideas of the work: it is the floor on which the individual persons move, practically confirming or contradicting those ideas in action and sentiment, subject to it as to the voice of the people and of God, and to its judicial authority and final sentence. In the oratorio-chorus the high significance of the Greek chorus has been far more fully realized than it ever can be in the opera-chorus."*

Such are the essential characteristics of the oratorio, into which a more detailed examination is unnecessary from the fact that this art-species in the form given it by HANDEL has been popularized and by frequent repetition been made accessible to all.** Former generations were in this regard not so fortunate: both HANDEL and BACH were soon after their death almost forgotten: the style of the Italian opera had about this time extended its dominion over church-music also, and its chief representatives

---

* See KOCH's Musical Lexicon, edited by A. VON DOMMER, article "Oratorio".

** This remark is especially true of that oratorio of HANDEL's which, from the very nature of its subject, appeals most strongly to the religious sensibilities of the multitude of protestant believers — the "Messiah", composed in 1741, in the short space of 24 days. "No musical work", says a writer in GROVE's *Dictionary of Music* — "has had such long, continuous, and enduring popularity as the Messiah, nor has any other so materially aided the cause of charity. Much of the veneration with which it is regarded is, doubtless, owing to the subject, but much also must be attributed to the splendid music, some of which .... is 'not for an age, but for all time'." (*Translator*.)

in Germany. GRAUN and HASSE, were praised as excellent models when BACH and HANDEL were mentioned, if at all, only as learned contrapuntists. Even MOZART became acquainted only by accident and in his later years with BACH's vocal compositions, on the occasion of a visit to Leipsic, where his friend DOLES, BACH's second successor as cantor at St. Thomas' church, had a motet of the old master sung for him as a rarity. It was only by the exertions of SCHEIBLE, founder of the St. Cecilia society at Frankfort, and of MENDELSSOHN, that an interest for BACH and HANDEL was, after a slumber of many generations, successfully re-awakened. The energy with which MENDELSSOHN, as youth of nineteen years, brought about the first performance of the revival of BACH's "Matthew-Passion" (Berlin, 1829), and the obstacles he had to overcome in so doing, are related at length by EDUARD DEVRIENT in his "Remembrances of MENDELSSOHN" ("Erinnerungen an F. MENDELSSOHN BARTHOLDY"). In a similar way MENDELSSOHN contributed, as director of the Lower-Rhine music-festivals, to the revival of the HANDEL oratorio. His loving reverence for these two masters was not, however, to go unrewarded, for it was their spirit that impelled him to the creation of his own most important works, the oratorios "St. Paul" and "Elijah".*

The "St. Paul" was begun in March, 1834, and finished at the beginning of 1836. It was first performed at Düsseldorf on Whitsunday, May 22, 1836; and in English, at Liverpool on Oct. 3 following. The "Elijah" was begun probably in 1838 (the score has no dates), and had its first performance in England, at the Birmingham Festival, Aug. 26, 1846, and in Germany, at Hamburg in October, 1847, under the direction of KREBS.**

* What follows of this section has been substituted for the few closing words of the original, as being it was thought of more general interest.
Translator.

** These two oratorios have repeatedly been performed in the United States, notably in New York, Boston and Cincinnati. The translator of this work has a vivid recollection of a scene connected with the introduction of "Elijah" into New York city, probably about the winter of 1846. The members of a vocal society directed by GEORGE LODER a native of Bath, England, and an excellent musician, who went from New York to California, where he died, were assembled one evening at their regular place of meeting, the Apollo Rooms, Broadway, in momentary expectation of the arrival of Mr. LODER with the pianoforte and vocal score of the "Elijah", of which we had heard so much.

In spite of the fact that after writing "St. Paul". MENDELSSOHN had the advantage, in the composition of "Elijah", of having, meanwhile, passed ten of the best years of his life in indefatigable work and the accumulation of a vast amount of experience, "yet it cannot be said" — says a writer in GROVE's Dictionary, under the title "Oratorio" — "that 'Elijah' is really a greater work than 'St. Paul': it is great in a different way. In one respect the main idea is the same as that treated in 'St. Paul' — the triumph of Truth over Falsehood. In both Oratorios the instrument by which this triumph is accomplished is a Heaven-commissioned Teacher, whose influence is distinctly perceptible throughout the entire work; only, in 'Elijah', the personality of this Teacher is more frequently brought before us than in 'St. Paul', where we are so frequently made to feel his influence without actually seeing him. As a natural consequence, the later Oratorio is much more dramatic in structure than the earlier one."

At last Mr. LODER appeared, in a state of delighted excitement and bearing the precious novelty, and seating himself at the piano gave us what I may call glimpses of the principal numbers of the work, which, though they were necessarily imperfect, created the greatest enthusiasm for the new oratorio, all the more as MENDELSSOHN's star was then in the ascendant.

Translator.

X.
INSTRUMENTAL MUSIC.

It is only cursorily that we have been able thus far to pay attention to instrumental music, and to call to mind its importance for musical development in general, especially for the cultivation of polyphonic music (see p. 27) and of modern opera (see p. 66). But after we have seen instrumental music grow up to be a co-ordinate power with vocal music, the time has come for making its evolutionary course also the subject of special consideration. In antiquity it is certainly not behind vocal music, at all events its origin reaches far beyond historic times. The invention of musical instruments resulted from the simplest of natural circumstances: the sun-dried intestines of a dead animal stretched across the skeleton occasioned the invention of *string-instruments*,* a broken reed, through which the wind breathed, that of *wind-instruments*. How these two principal species were in use in antiquity, and that in various sub-species, partly as solo instruments, partly united in an orchestra, has been mentioned in the proper place. As regards wind-instruments, however, we must here lay stress on a peculiarity of their gradual development, a phenomenon which we shall have occasion in the farther course of the history of instrumental music to consider once more, viz: that their development, as culture advances, proceeds from the complex to the simple: the oldest wind-instrument is the "Pan's-pipes" (the "Syrinx" of the Greeks), formed of many

---

* According to Greek tradition it was a tortoise, the appearance of which in this condition suggested to the god Hermes as he walked by the sea-shore the idea of the Lyre.

reeds, later the "Double-flute" appears, and when the antique civilization reaches its climax, the simple Flute attains the supremacy.

During the Middle Age, besides the traditional musical instruments those with *keys* and *bows* were also in use, especially among the Northern nations, yet were on so low a plane of development as to be utterly unfitted for rendering artistic musicforms like those that had already then developed themselves in vocal music. The first instrument to serve higher artistic purposes was the *Organ*; by the very consequence of its relationship to the church it was in the hands of eminent and learned musicians at a time when the other instruments were exclusively given over to itinerant players or afterwards to the town-musicians. During the first centuries after its introduction into the church it was, on account of its awkward mechanism, certainly ill calculated to contribute to the dignity of divine service. An English historian, the monk WULSTON, writes in the year 951 of an organ built for Winchester Cathedral having four hundred pipes and thirteen pairs of bellows, the latter requiring seventy men to blow them: yet as the instrument had but ten tones, forty pipes being under the control of each key, evidently the chief aim must have been the attainment of the greatest possible power. It was not much better with the organs afterwards built at Halberstadt, Magdeburg and Erfurt, whose keys were a hand broad and could be pressed down only by the fist or even the elbows. The Brunswick music-director MICHAEL PRÆTORIUS, whose "Syntagma musicum", published in 1615, contains in the section entitled "Organographie" important information about the instruments of former times, says of these organs that for the kind of music then in use one could make out very well with them, "seeing that no composition with many voices but only the simple monophonic choral was played on them". With this the organists were satisfied until singers had begun to sound various tone-series simultaneously (see p. 28 and the organ also on its part wished to enjoy the advantages of polyphonic music. It was of course impossible to play in parallel Fifths and Octaves, after the manner of the "Organum", as the stiffness of the touch did not allow more than one key at a time to be played: this was remedied, however, by so uniting several pipes tuned in Fifths and Octaves that they could all be simultaneously sounded by means of one key. These so-called *Mixtures*, which have been retained to this day, must have had at first a barbarous effect: but in the modern organ the symphonous* Fifths and Octaves are so subdued that our ear does not recognize them as independent tones but merely as an integration and re-inforcement of the melody.

Improvement in organ-playing went of course hand in hand with that of the instrument: its first evolution as also its final perfection it found in Germany, where we meet at an early date two artists of great merit for the cultivation of the technic of organ-playing: BERNHARD MURER, probably identical with BERNARD THE GERMAN, engaged at St. Mark's, Venice, in 1470, and regarded as the inventor of organ-pedals, and the organist of St. Sebaldus, Nürnberg, CONRAD PAUMANN or PAULMANN, born blind, died at Munich in 1473. Subsequently Italy becomes the real seat of organ-playing, Venice especially, after the most famous organist of his time, CLAUDIO MERULO, was appointed principal organist of St. Mark's, in that city. But Italian organ-playing reaches its climax in Rome with GIROLAMO FRESCOBALDI, from 1615 organist of St. Peter's in that city, whose art had such fascination that his admirers followed him in his journeys from city to city, and ambitious organists of all countries sought his instruction. After him and his likewise famous pupil PASQUINI, organ-playing in Italy, whose powers were just now entirely taken up with the cultivation of dramatic music, falls into a decline and blossoms again in Germany, where SAMUEL SCHEIDT (died in 1654 as organist of the church of St. Maurice at Halle, his native city) begins the series of illustrious organists in which the names of FROBERGER, PACHELBEL, BUXTEHUDE, REINKEN, lastly SEBASTIAN BACH appear as shining lights. All these worked not only as virtuosos but also as composers for their instrument and became creators of a peculiar style of instrumental music whose development, in view of the already mentioned specially honorable position of the organ, necessarily followed from this as a

---

* We have no word in English exactly corresponding to the German "mitklingend", literally, "together-sounding". I have therefore ventured to coin, from the Greek, the word "symphonous", which exactly expresses the meaning of the German word. See my *Primer of Modern Tonality*, first foot-note, page 15.) *Translator.*

logical consequence. The essential features of this style might be recognized at once in the works of the afore-mentioned masters; but for better understanding the style as also the instrumental music-forms that attained development at the same time with it, let us previously consider the evolutionary process of the other instruments, especially of the pianoforte, which at quite an early period took a similar exceptional position among the instruments to that of the organ, after it had proved itself to be as well and even better adapted than the latter to the representation of musical thoughts and forms of the most different kind.

The origin of the keyed *string*-instruments is traced to two primitive instruments — the *Monochord* and the *Psaltery*. The former consisted of a long, narrow four-cornered sound-box with *one* string (as the Greek name implies), which by means of a movable bridge could be divided up according to a diagram of proportionate lengths marked under it. This instrument served in antiquity as also in the Middle Age for the determination of the tone-relationships (intervals) and for the first instruction in music. In the course of time, in order to dispense with the shifting of the bridge, keys were adapted to one of the sides of the box, to the lever-ends of which brass pins were fixed, so that, the key being pressed down, the pins would rise and at the same time divide the string and make it sound.* After the addition of more strings, the Monochord became in the 12th or 13th century the *Clavichord*, which, however, preserved up to the most recent times the memory of its origin, the number of its strings being smaller, even despite the continuous improvement of the instrument, than that of its tones and the keys corresponding to them. Until 1725, from which time the clavichord began to dispense with frets, one and the same string, struck at a smaller or greater distance from the bridge, served for two tones, the diatonic tone and the chromatic half-step above it, so that a simultaneous sounding of both these tones was impossible.

Over against the Clavichord stand the key-instruments derived from the Psaltery, viz: the *Harpsichord* Clavicembalo, Cem-

---

* The shorter part of the string, not intended to be sounded, does indeed give a tone also, but so weak as to be quite covered up by that of the longer part.

balo) and its varieties the *Spinet* and *Virginal*, this last name having been conferred in England, in honor of the Virgin Queen Elisabeth, as some say, more probably because the instrument played an important part in the education of young women. The instruments of the harpsichord, clavicembalo or spinet family differed from the clavichord in that they were constructed on the *plectrum* principle, *i. e.*, "the strings were set in motion by points of quill or hard leather elevated on wooden uprights known as 'jacks', and twitching or plucking them as the depression of the keys caused the points to pass upwards. Leather points were probably used first, since we learn from SCALIGER, who lived 1484—1550, that crowquills were introduced in key-instruments subsequent to his boyhood, and he informs us that through them the name 'spinet' from *spina*, a thorn or point) became applied to what had been known as the 'clavicymbal' and 'harpsichord'."[*] The clearness of tone resulting from this principle, to which fulness also was not wanting after the harpsichord had become polychordal, in the sense of having two or more strings to each tone, fitted the instrument for coöperation with the orchestra, and it remained till after HANDEL's time a valued support in larger vocal and instrumental performances. Such advantages the clavichord, with its gentle, transparent tone-quality, of course could not claim, but on the other hand it was much better adapted for reproducing the psychic subject-matter of a piece of music and bringing out its fine points. BACH is said to have preferred the clavichord to the pianoforte, and BEETHOVEN to have expressed himself to the effect that "the clavichord among all key-instruments was that on which one could best control tone and expressive interpretation".

Notwithstanding the importance of piano-playing in the 17th and still more in the beginning of the 18th century, the technics of the art remained on an extremely low plane up to BACH's time. Special difficulty was found in the treatment of the thumb, which for centuries was employed merely for stretching larger intervals, whilst in scales and passages it could be put to no better use than supporting the fingers engaged — generally only the third and fourth, — sliding meanwhile to and fro on a board

---

[*] GROVE's *Dictionary of Music*, Part VI, article "Harpsichord".

placed below the key-board. How little stress was laid upon a systematic fingering is seen in the assertion of Prætorius, that "it makes no difference whether this or that fingering be used: make your runs with whatever fingers you choose, even use your nose for it, so long as everything is made to sound well and correct", etc. — and more than a century afterward Mattheson writes, in his "School of Thorough bass" (Hamburg, 1731): "As many as there are players, almost so many kinds of fingering will you find. One runs with four fingers, another with five, some even — and almost as fast — with only two. It is of no consequence, so long as one adopts a certain rule and sticks to it". In this connection we will not omit to mention the merits that the French, besides the Germans and Italians, have acquired in developing piano-playing. Especially after the close of the 17th century this art was lovingly cherished by the French organists, among them Louis Marchand born 1669, a master in brilliant and elegant playing, though he felt obliged to decline entering into a musical rivalry with Sebastian Bach on meeting him at Dresden; then, his pupil Rameau, already alluded to as opera-composer and theoretician; lastly François Couperin (born 1668), the famous member of a numerous family of artists of this name, whose fine and elegant compositions, though occasionally overloaded with embellishments, determined the direction of the piano-playing of his time and were highly esteemed even by Sebastian Bach. To the efforts of this artist in the department of the purely technical his "L'art de toucher le clavecin", published in 1716 at Paris, gives brilliant testimony. The fingering here recommended already points to a more frequent use of the thumb, though it would seem that it was not before Bach that all the fingers had been trained to an equal development. How greatly the development of the technics of piano-playing in other respects was promoted by Bach, is seen partly from his compositions, partly also from the instruction-book of his son and pupil Carl Philipp Emanuel Bach, "Essay on the true manner of playing the pianoforte" (Berlin, 1759), which summarizes all the experiences made up to that time, and starting out from them effects the transition to modern pianoforte-playing.

Little as Emanuel Bach is to be compared in depth and creative power with his father, he still deserves a prominent place in the history of instrumental music, and the honors paid to him as virtuoso and composer by his contemporaries were by no means undeserved. In his various spheres of action, from 1740 to 1767 as chamber-pianist to Frederick the Great and music-director to the princess Amelia of Prussia, then until his death in 1788 as music-director at Hamburg, he was counted an authority of the first rank, especially in the domain of pianoforte-playing. "He is the father, we are the youngsters", said MOZART in an assembly, when his playing was spoken of: "whoever of us can do anything right learned it of him; and he who will not acknowledge this is a —". HAYDN, too, recognized in his last years the merits of the older master in the words: "He who knows me thoroughly must find that I owe very much to EMANUEL BACH, that I have understood him and diligently studied him; he himself once paid me a compliment about it". For the present time EMANUEL BACH's compositions have, as genuine expressions of the taste of his time, characterized as it was by sickly sentimentality, lost most of their effect. Yet his influence on the pianoforte-playing of that time must have been the greater for the reason that he marks the transition, from the practice of the older composers who left the details of embellishment almost entirely to the executant, to that of the later ones, by whom everything referring to the delivery is with great minuteness prescribed to the player.

In spite of all the efforts of the older masters of the pianoforte thus far named, the instrument would hardly have attained its present importance in musical life had a mechanism not been invented by whose means the tone could sound in various degrees of power, which was not the case with either the clavichord or the harpsichord. The first impulse to the invention of such a mechanism was given by the DULCIMER, made by a certain PANTALEON HEBENSTREIT at the end of the 17th century, after the manner of the cymbal, and struck with hammers in the hand. The advantage here of being able to strike the strings powerfully, or softly at pleasure, suggested to the Paduan CRISTOFALI or CRISTOFORI), about 1710, the idea of providing the upper ends of the keys of the harpsichord with hammers, to spring up from below against the strings and to rebound immediately after the stroke. Soon afterward he perfected his invention by a contrivance for damping, which suppresses the sound of the string the moment the finger is raised from the key. The instrument so constructed, which was called in Italy *Piano-forte*, as admitting of soft or loud playing at pleasure, made on its appearance no small sensation and was immediately imitated and improved by the harpsichord-makers of that time. Some of these, as MARIUS in Paris and the organist SCHRÖTER at Nordhausen, even disputed with CRISTOFALI the honor of the invention, yet it has recently been shown that it was not till five or six years later that they publicly exhibited their models. Some twenty-five years after its introduction into Italy the piano-forte, having been improved by SILBERMANN (died at Dresden in 1756), became known in Germany; yet it did not succeed in supplanting the keyed string-instruments in use at that time until a pupil of SILBERMANN's, JOHANN ANDREAS STEIN, of Augsburg, had in the last quarter of the preceding century raised the instrument to that degree of perfection that made it capable of giving fit expression to the new spirit of music that meanwhile had awakened.

Still another instrument of musico-historical importance was supplanted by the piano-forte — the *Lute*, which had for centuries held a scarcely less prominent place in musical life than the clavichord or the harpsichord. It was first introduced into Europe (Spain) by the Arabs, its name being derived from the Arabic *al oud*, the shell. Its shape, suggestive of the shell of the tortoise, confirms this origin, and at the same time its affinity to the most ancient string-instrument of the Greeks, invented according to tradition by the god Hermes. The strings of the lute, which were plucked by the fingers, lay partly *over* partly *beside* the finger-board; their number varied with the different patterns of the instrument, of which at PRAETORIUS' time seven were in use, from the *theorbo*, which had a very long neck and was used in Italy for song-accompaniment, and the similar great octave bass-lute, down to the treble, small treble and small octave-lute. The lute was employed not only for accompanying solo and chorus-singing, but also as a solo and orchestral instrument, and it was at home everywhere, both at church and in opera, but most especially in private circles. It has an extensive literature, beginning with CONRAD PAUMANN (see p. 124), who invented for it a peculiar notation, the German *Tablature*,* so-called, according

---

* The word *Tablature* from the Latin *tabula*, table denotes not only

to which the strings lying over the finger-board are indicated by German letters, the open strings lying near them by figures, and the note-values by the stems and tails ˋˋ˃ of modern notation. The following, from a book by HANS GERLE (Nürnberg, 1532), is an example of a folk-song* in lute-tablature with a transcription in modern notation.

The literature of this instrument does not appear to have come to an end until the time of JOHANN ADAM HILLER (see p. 98), whose operettas were still printed in an arrangement for the lute, yet even then its popularity had greatly diminished. MATTHESON, as early as the first quarter of the preceding century, formally declares war against the lute and blames especially the superficiality of its "professors", moreover its "insinuating tone-quality, which always promises more than it performs", finally the difficulty also of properly tuning it. This must indeed have been

---

the whole body of the art-rules current among the Master-singers (see p. 43), but also what we now call *score* (vocal or orchestral, or simply, in the case of monophonic music, *notation*. There were two kinds of tablature for the lute — the German and the Italian, the latter consisting of a system of six lines, on which the frets were indicated by ciphers. This system was introduced into Germany also about the year 1600. Besides the above there is also what was called an *organ-tablature* for key-instruments, a method of indicating tones by letters, as represented in my *Primer of Modern Tonality*, p. 12, Fig. 4.   *Translator.*

* It has been arranged by ROBERT FRANZ under the title: "Ach Elslein, liebes Elselein".

almost insuperable, as the strings lying over the finger-board were doubled, while those lying next to them, as they could not be shortened, necessarily got out of tune with every change of key. Besides, the smallness and weakness of the whole instrument was not rightly proportioned to the number of strings, especially when their number had increased in the course of time to twenty-four, fourteen *over* and ten *beside* the finger-board.

The species of *bow* and *wind-instruments* were in the earlier ages far more numerous than now. The former are to be traced as to their origin either to the Keltic *Crotta*, called by the mediæval writers *Rota* or *Rotte*, or to the Arabic *Rebec*, afterwards the favorite instrument of the Troubadours. In mediæval Latin these instruments were named, after the word *fides* (a gut-string), *fidula* or *vidula*, which expression, variously corrupted, led through the intermediate forms *figella*, *vielle* and *viocl* to the Italian "viola" and English "fiddle" and "viol". At the beginning of the Middle Age we find the viola in two species: the *viola da gamba* (leg-violin) and the *viola da braccia* (arm-violin), which are again subdivided into thirteen sub-species, corresponding to the various registers of the human voice. This is explained by the fact that far beyond the Middle Age there was no independent instrumental music and the instruments had to be satisfied, if they were to participate at all in artistic music, with simply doubling the voice-parts of polyphonic vocal compositions. As the bow-instruments accordingly were grouped in bass, tenor, alto and treble viols, so too the wind-instruments formed each for itself a similar family in various grades, the older wood wind-instruments the *bombard* and *shawm* being specially rich in sub-species affording collectively the compass of five and a half octaves.

This variety still existed in the 17th century, at the time of PRÆTORIUS. Meanwhile an entirely new field of activity was opened for instrumental music; after MONTEVERDE had recognized and taught how to consider the individuality of each separate instrument, the time came when a *return from multiplicity to simplicity* became necessary, and the majority of the instruments till then in use had to make way for some few that were best adapted for solving the higher art-problems that henceforth were propounded. Of the bow-instruments but four species conquered in the struggle for existence: the *bass-viola* and the tenor *viola da* *gamba* passed over into the modern orchestra as *contrabasso* and *violoncello* respectively; so too the tenor viola as simply *viola*, and the treble viola as *violin* (Italian *violino*, the termination "*ino*" being diminutive). In the same proportion the number of wind-instruments was reduced; out of the many kinds of the cross-flute (flauto traverso) and the beak-flute (flûte à bec), which latter is not held across the lips but straight out, and is blown by means of a mouth-piece like a bird's beak, only the modern *flute* and *clarinet* were retained. From the shawm was developed the *oboe*, which at first (about 1700) also appears in various sizes, but at the golden age of instrumental music exists in only one form. Of the bombard finally there remained but the bass-bombard, which, after its long, unwieldy tube had been changed into a double tube like a fagot was called in Italian *fagotto*, in English *bassoon*.* Of the instruments which in time have wholly disappeared, we will mention here the *cornet* only (in the old sense of the word), a wind-instrument of wood covered with black leather, in some species straight in form, in others crooked. On account of its clear and penetrating tone it was extensively used in church-music and by town-musicians, also for sounding the melodies of chorals from church-towers, as late as the beginning of the 18th century.

It is easily conceivable that the smaller the number of varieties of instruments the greater could be the care bestowed on their construction. *Violin-making* begins to flourish in Italy as early as 1600, Cremona having among all cities made for itself a special name in this regard. Here at first labored the family AMATI, whose progenitor ANTONIO (1592—1619) gave bow-instruments the form that they have in spite of all attempted improvements retained to this day. If, notwithstanding, Cremona violin-making in the last quarter of the 17th century was able through ANDREA, GIUSEPPE and PIETRO GUARNERI, also ANTON STRADIVARI, to make progress, still the construction of the

---

* "There is reason to believe that the bassoon is of Eastern origin: . . . . The Egyptian word for a pipe of deep tone * * * * is, according to E. W. LANE ('Modern Egyptians'), *Zummarah-bi-soan*, and the manner in which the word *Buzaine, Buisine,* is used in mediæval MSS., shows a possible connection with this origin." STAINER and BARRETT's *Dictionary of Musical terms*, article "Bassoon".   *Translator.*

instrument did not undergo at the hands of these masters any essential alteration. It is different with wind-instruments, which have up to the latest hour experienced (through ADOLPH SAX in Paris' transformative improvements. That epoch was however a specially important one for the development of wind-instruments also: the flute — for instance — owes many an improvement to JOHANN JOACHIM QUANZ (1697—1773), court-composer and teacher of Frederick the Great, he having before his call to Berlin earnestly devoted himself to the improvement of its mechanism and afterwards (1752) published his experiences in a valuable monograph: "Attempt at a method of playing the cross-flute."

The necessary consequence of the increasing independence of the instruments was their emancipation from vocal music, and the development of a style in keeping with their capacities, as also of the music-forms resulting therefrom. The *instrumental style* is distinguished from the vocal essentially by greater rhythmical precision as also by greater flexibility. The former attribute it owes to the dance, for accompanying which the instruments were seen to be by their very nature better adapted than the human voice, which for evident reasons, such as the necessity of drawing breath, and of a distinct pronunciation of the text, etc., was unable to adapt itself with perfect ease to the movements of the dancers. This did not hinder it, however, from associating itself with the dance in antiquity and even far into the Middle Age, until at last the instruments had sufficiently advanced in their development to take sole possession of dance-music, and, while retaining the song-form, to carry out still farther the independent culture of that dance-tune,* the *Hyporchema* of the ancients. — The greater flexibility of the instrumental style lay also in the very nature of the instruments, and showed itself at an early date in the necessity they were under of dividing up the

---

* The primitive identity of dance-music with song is commemorated by the technical term "Song-form" in German, "*Liedform*",, which is applied in an enlarged sense, as comprising the structure also of the different varieties of pieces composed for dancing. With a view to greater exactness of terminology, however, the expression "Primary form" has been recommended to take the place of "Song-form". See my "Theory and Practice of Musical Form, on the basis of LUDWIG BUSSLER's Formenlehre" (published by G. SCHIRMER, New York), Chapter VI. *Translator.*

long-sustained tones of song into smaller parts, which was called "diminishing", "coloring" or "varying". In this, too, instrumental music had for the time being kept pace with song, as long, that is, as the "art of organating" was practised by singers with the unconstraint alluded to on page 45. But when the singers, as we saw at the same place, went back, as polyphonic music became more and more developed, to the sustained style of composition, the instruments began to cultivate all the more zealously the "diminishing", etc. henceforth given over to them exclusively, and the immediate result of their efforts in this direction was the rise of special instrumental music-forms, of which the *Toccata* is the oldest. In this species of composition the last-mentioned peculiarity of style has full play, inasmuch as here instead of the sustained melody running and broken figures predominate, into which the harmony is decomposed. It owes its artistic form to the Venetian organist CLAUDIO MERULO (see p. 124), who published in 1598 his first Toccatas; it obtained its perfect development through FRESCOBALDI, whose Toccatas include all the musical achievements of his time: the fugue, free imitation, brilliant passage-work and mighty torrents of chord-successions.

What is called *cantabile* playing, over against the figured style of the Toccata, came into prominence in a second art-form, the *Canzone*, in name as in its nature a transformation of the French *chanson*. It also hails from Venice, where JOHANNES GABRIELI (from the end of the 16th century on) published a large number of such compositions. Still greater acknowledgments are due this artist for procuring the participation of the bow-instruments and wind-instruments in the improvements that had been made, after composers had up to that time devoted all their efforts to key-instruments exclusively. The independent orchestral pieces composed by GABRIELI are, to be sure, of the most modest dimensions; their entire length amounts to from twelve to twenty measures, and they had but one aim, either as "Symphony" to introduce a vocal piece, or as "Ritornello" (interlude), to fill up the pauses enabling the singer to rest. Similar is the case with the *Sonata*, which likewise appears about this time; its name originally means nothing more than an instrumental piece, as is shown by the very title of GABRIELI's work (published in 1586):

"Sonata a cinque per istromenti",* and by the words of Prætorius: "Sonata (from *sonando*) is so called because the performance is not with human voices but with instruments only." If moreover we read in the same author that "the word 'sonata' or 'sonada' is applied to the flourish of trumpets for calling to meals or to the dance," we may calculate the enormous distance that separates that music-form from the modern complex sonata.

The complex or *cyclical* instrumental music-forms are however by no means of recent date: in the earliest days of town-musicians and musical guilds it was customary to perform a number of dance-tunes, united in a series or cycle, without the dance that belonged to them. The dance-tunes thus strung together, in other respects having no other inter-connection than community of key, were at first called in Italian *Partita*, and soon excited the attention of players of key-instruments, especially of the French, under whose hands the Partita was raised to the dignity of the *Suite*. As such it went back to Germany, where, as is well known, it was developed by BACH to the utmost possible perfection, yet without drawing near to the modern sonata, which essentially differs from the suite in this, that its several movements have organic coherence one with another. The impulse to the development of this artistically immeasurably higher cyclical form was given by the tripartite opera-overture in the form it had acquired in Italy through A. SCARLATTI, in France through LULLI. It has been already remarked, in speaking of the former artist, that this overture, after its movements had been separated and enlarged, and inwardly perfected for performance at concerts, led over into the modern orchestral symphony. As an intermediate stage in this evolution we may regard the solo violin-sonata of many movements developed in Italy, especially by CORELLI (died in 1713): also the concerto of three movements introduced by the Venetian violinist VIVALDI (died 1743). Already here the cyclical form appears perfectly developed, as is proved by SEBAS-

---

* This title is moreover characteristic of the primitive condition of the instrumental music of that date: up to MONTEVERDE's time composers did not assign to each instrument a special part in keeping with its character, but were content to write out the voice-parts of an orchestral movement, leaving it to the director to fill them, according to their compass, with the instruments that he happened to have at his disposal.

tian Bach's "Italian concerto" for clavichord, which may be regarded as a model for the modern sonata-form. That the master who was creative in so many provinces of his art did not feel called upon to transfer this form to the pianoforte, but was satisfied with this single attempt, is all the more difficult to understand from the fact that the need of such a transference had in many ways manifested itself already before his time.

Johann Kuhnau, Bach's predecessor as precentor at St. Thomas' church at Leipsic, had first ventured on the attempt, yet without being clearly conscious of the importance of this step. In the preface to his work entitled "Clavier-exercises", etc., published 1695, he excuses his attempt in the words: "Why should such things not be done on the clavier just as on other instruments, since no single instrument has ever disputed with the clavier the precedence in perfection?" Yet the new art-species seems to have been favorably received on the part of the piano-forte players, for soon afterwards Kuhnau published a collection of seven sonatas. With scarcely less right than Kuhnau can Domenico Scarlatti (1683—1757) claim the paternity of the piano-forte sonata, for, though he went back to the one-movement form, yet in this movement the form of the first movement of our modern sonata is already distinctly imprinted. Scarlatti's special merit, however, is that he brought in vogue a new method of composition adapted to the piano-forte, by introducing, in place of the *polyphonic* style with its perfect equality of all the parts, from which neither Kuhnau nor Bach could break loose, the *homophonic*, in which essentially one voice, carrying the melody, is the ruling one, while the other voices are merely secondary, as forming the accompaniment. This advance marks at the same time the separation of piano-forte playing from organ playing, which had until then hardly been distinguished one from the other. True, the author of the first organ and piano-forte school, published 1593 in Venice, Pater Girolamo Diruta, a pupil of Merulo, had called attention to the difference in the technical treatment of these two instruments, yet the subsequent composers had disregarded his admonitions and gone on, as before, writing for key-instruments in general.

Nor did Domenico Scarlatti yet recognize the real significance of the piano-forte sonata, but commended his sonatas to the indulgence of the public with the remark that "in them not deep design would be found but the ingenious pleasantry of art". In fact, he makes more account of technics than of intellectual contents: yet by his application of the principle of tripartition, prescriptive for the modern sonata, and by a number of effective innovations of a technical kind, such as running passages in thirds and sixths, the quick stroke of one and the same key with different fingers, broken chords in contrary motion for both hands, etc., he leads us directly into the modern age. The piano-forte sonata afterwards appears fully developed with EMANUEL BACH, from whose hands it was received by the great masters of instrumental music, first HAYDN (1732—1809), then MOZART (1756—1791), by both of whom the form established by EM. BACH was preserved. It was reserved to BEETHOVEN (1770—1827) to carry out these forms to the extremest limits of their expansibility, and thereby to adapt them for receiving the new spirit in music awakened by him. Through him also the *orchestral symphony* attained to full maturity: its evolutionary course need not here be described, as it essentially coïncides with that of the sonata. We merely mention as chief points its transformation from the three-movement form of the Italian overture to that of four movements by the addition of the *Minuet* from the suite, as also the change of this dance-piece into the now passionate now humorous *Scherzo* dating from BEETHOVEN.

The brilliant and dominant epoch of instrumental music beginning with these last-named masters is conditionated, in the same degree as the blossoming of the Passion and the Oratorio brought about by the earlier generation of composers, by the *idealistic world-view* that in Germany has always, but especially since the re-awakening of the popular consciousness after the Thirty Years' War, been the characteristic feature of the intellectual life. For, instrumental composition affords to the creative musician far greater liberty to rise to the supersensual than vocal composition, which with its dependence on external conditions marks under all circumstances certain limits to the flight of his imagination. Now, just as the conception of music that came to the surface in Germany during the preceding century is contrary to that entertained by the neighboring nations, especially the French, so too *German philosophy*, after it had simultaneously with music and led by the same inclination to idealism, entered upon a new epoch. If Englishmen and Frenchmen had indicated the sensual impressions as sole source of human knowledge and consequently the former had evolved therefrom *Sensualism*, the latter *Materialism*, the German *Idealism* finds the essential conditions of all knowledge in the human spirit itself; and if the former aim at materializing all that is spiritual, the German philosophy everywhere strives after a spiritualization of matter. This is seen in LEIBNITZ, the father of modern German philosophy, who conceives substance, *e. g.*, not — with his predecessors — as an aggregate of lifeless atoms but of intellectually animated individuals, called by him *monads*. The climax of this philosophy is reached by IMMANUEL KANT, who through his "Criticism of pure reason", published in 1781, arrives at the result that besides the sensuous impressions certain *a priori* conceptions in the human mind — as, for instance, of space, and time — are necessary for knowledge. If we cannot rise by means of pure reason to the supersensuous, KANT's "Criticism of practical reason" (1788) shows us the way in which this demand of our spiritual nature also is satisfied. Practical reason desires the suppression of the sensuous man by means of the reasonable man, which latter gives a law to the former; but this law, unlike the maxims of prudence, is not conditionated upon the prospect of certain successes, but is an absolute, the only absolute commandment — KANT calls it the *categorical imperative*. It is practical reason also that leads to certain claims, not indeed logically demonstrable but for all that indispensable, called by KANT *postulates*. As such he indicates the *freedom of the will*, because the will must be independent of natural necessity in order that it may follow the voice of the categorical imperative; *immortality*, because despite the imperfection of human nature the possibility of a continual approach to the condition of moral perfection must be assumed; finally the *existence of God*, because in nature there is no necessary connection between morality and a happiness proportioned to it, and the realisation of this agreement, as of the highest good, must be guaranteed by a being having on the one hand absolute power over nature, whilst on the other hand it is influenced simply by moral impulses.

KANT's technology, contained in his "Criticism of the judicial faculty", published in 1790, is concerned with the Beautiful, which we estimate by taste, by means of the feeling of pleasure (the esthetic judicial faculty), as opposed to the Congruous inherent in organic nature, which we judge by intellect and reason (the teleological judicial faculty). The esthetic judicial faculty* enables us to recognize the *Beautiful* as that which by means of its form, harmonizing with the human intellect, excites general and necessary pleasure; the *Sublime* as the simply Great, which evokes in us the idea of the Infinite and by its antagonism to the interests of the senses directly pleases. These definitions, as also that of the Beautiful as *symbol of the morally Good*, were farther carried out especially by SCHILLER in his esthetic treatises, as KANT's Ethics were by FICHTE. In the warm, enthusiastic presentation of these two men the Kantian philosophy soon became the common property of the German nation and caused a mighty revolution in all provinces of the intellectual life. Under its inspiration the German masters of musical art also were enabled, with the sole aid of absolute music to win the victory over Italian opera, all-powerful as it then was and surrounded by the other arts as vassals. The orchestral instruments, which had till then amused themselves with the harmless performance of suites, divertissements, serenades, etc., began now, united in the *symphony*, to speak a language of deepest seriousness. "HAYDN was", as RICHARD WAGNER says in his "Zukunftsmusik" (Music of the future), "the genial master that first developed this form into broader dimensions, and through inexhaustible variety of motives and of

---

* *Esthetics*, literally the science of the sensuous perceptions and feelings, in a narrower sense the science of the Beautiful — *i. e.*, the Beautiful in *art* as opposed to the Beautiful in *nature* — owes its introduction as a science to the philosopher ALEXANDER BAUMGARTEN, whose monograph "Aesthetica" (1750) gave it its name. Among the estheticians of antiquity — for the nature of the Beautiful and of art has of course been at all times a subject of philosophical investigation — ARISTOTLE claims the attention of the musician especially, in so far as he allots to music a prominent place among the arts. All art attains its end, the ennoblement of the mind and the heart, by imitation Mimesis), yet not of visible nature but of the movements of the human character (Ethos) and soul (Psyche), which movements music (as ARISTOTLE explains in his "Politics", Book VIII, chap. 5) *directly* represents, whereas the plastic arts can only give through forms Schemata, *certain signs* of the esthetic occurrences.

their connections and exploitations gave it a deeply expressive significance. MOZART had recognized the charm, previously unknown to the German masters, of Italian song-melody, and, while he introduced into Italian opera the richer development of the German method of instrumental composition, imparted in turn to the orchestral melody the full euphony of the Italian song-method. Into the rich, much-promising heritage of both these masters BEETHOVEN entered; he developed the symphonic art-work into so fascinating a breadth of form, and filled this form with a so extraordinarily varied and captivating melodic content, that at this day we stand before the Beethovenian symphony as before the boundary-stone of a quite new period of art-history in general; for with it a phenomenon made its appearance to which the art of no other period and no other nation can show anything even only approximately analogous. Inasmuch as here music speaks a language that with its free and bold conformity to law must seem to us more powerful than all logic, while yet rational thought holding on to the clew of cause and effect finds here no foothold. BEETHOVEN's symphony must appear to us directly as a revelation from another world."

It is easily conceivable that in consequence of so unexpectedly high a leap of instrumental music, the musical world after BEETHOVEN turned to cultivating it with a zeal that was pushed to one-sidedness. Yet it was not granted to the musical Romanticists of the 19th century, as far as they followed after BEETHOVEN, to come up to their model, much less to surpass it. Only those composers who turned their attention to what BEETHOVEN had neglected — the opera — were able with the aid of the orchestral means bequeathed by him to help this art-species to blossom anew, and thus also to protect music in general from the imminent danger of stagnation.

XI.

THE ROMANTICISTS OF THE 19ᵀᴴ CENTURY.

The conception "classical", with which we associate the idea of a cheerful, naive, peaceful state of mind, has for its antithesis "romantic", an expression applied in an art-sense to a period when the more serious part of humanity, dissatisfied with the existing state of things, yearns to be out of the actual world and strives after remote, obscurely beheld ideals. Now, it is true that this inclination to rise above prosy reality has been at all times and everywhere a mark of intellectually gifted and poetic natures, and accordingly Romanticism is essentially synonymous with poetry and as old as the world itself. Yet at certain times and among certain peoples the romantic impulse manifests itself with unusual power. The ancient Greeks, living more exteriorly than interiorly, scarcely knew it and certainly did not foster it; the son of the North, on the contrary, loved to descend into his interior, being already admonished by the prudery and harshness of his climate to build for himself a special imaginary world in place of the real world about him. Here too, however, we distinguish between epochs that were more or less favorable to romanticism: its flowering-time coincides with the periods in which humanity, after important political and social revolutions, finds the attendant disillusions specially galling, *e. g.*, the centuries after the collapse of the antique world with its rich intellectual culture, and in later times the first decennaries of our century. The enthusiasm kindled by the epoch of enlightenment of FREDERICK THE GREAT, then by the French revolution, lastly by the deliverance of Europe from the yoke of NAPOLEON, necessarily gave way to profound discouragement and insipidity after the temporary failure of all these efforts was acknowledged, and thus it came to pass that then even the most gifted natures turned aside hopelessly from what was to them the insipid reality, to betake themselves to a far distant phantom-existence.

When this intellectual current got the upper hand it was unavoidable that art should be forced away from the path of development trodden in the century that had elapsed, and that the rich artistic harvest of that period should again be called in question. Only in certain directions could the march of time, the dawning aspiration after unattainable ideals lead to positive achievements: primarily in the domain of lyric poetry, which under the influence of the dominant mood was just now experiencing a significant enlargement of its sphere of action. In place of the general subject-matter with which the lyric poetry of the preceding century had been satisfied, the subjective feelings of the poet now came to the front, and the essential nature of lyric poetry, a boundless submersion into the innermost life of the soul, could under these circumstances attain full prominence. It was that universality of subject-matter that had hitherto prevented lyric poetry from accomplishing its true mission, *i. e.*, from operating, as it had done in antiquity, in the closest conjunction with music. Not without success had JOHANN FRIEDRICH REICHARDT (from 1775 on music-director to FREDERICK THE GREAT), C. F. ZELTER (from 1800 till his death in 1832 director of the Berlin Academy for Singing), and others exerted themselves in artistically developing the German song. For the reason just given, however, their efforts did not avail to bring about a substantial progress, and even such masters as MOZART and BEETHOVEN, in view of the then state of lyric poetry, did not draw from the latter that deep inspiration that might have induced them to interest themselves fully in song-composition. But under the influence of romanticism subjective lyric poetry was enabled to find new forms and richer subject-matter; it put forth glorious blossoms that notwithstanding their dazzling brilliancy of color and occasionally strange odor, never denied their rise from the very depths of the German heart. At the same time too the tongue of music was loosed, so that the long desired transformation of the folk-song into the art-song could be accomplished, and from this time forth the victory of the German song over the Italian *bravura* air was assured.

The difference between the *folk-song* and the *art-song* is essentially this, that in the former one and the same melody answers for each strophe, whereas in the art-song the music most closely attaches itself to the poem throughout its entire course, regardless of the strophical divisions, and endeavors to illustrate its subject-matter even in the smallest particulars. This song-species[*] is farther distinguished from the popular strophic song by its accompaniment, which maintains a much higher degree of independence, sometimes even temporarily supplying the place of the silent voice. In the folk-song, on the contrary, the accompaniment seems to grow of itself out of the melody, whose harmonic and rhythmic proportions are its only rule, except that it may by breaking (arpeggiating) the chords enliven the movement to a certain extent. Naturally, the German song-poem in its new form disclosed to the fantasy of the composer an immense sphere of creation; but to occupy it and rule it with genial freedom no one was found worthier than FRANZ SCHUBERT, who is therefore rightly honored as the creator of the German art-song.

Hardly would this artistic achievement of SCHUBERT's have so perfectly succeeded, if his extraordinary musical talent had not been accompanied by a rare natural strength and simplicity, if what was temperate and harmonious in his artist-nature had not restrained him from the excesses of the romantic tendency, from which even his great predecessor BEETHOVEN was not free. That the arbitrarinesses in which the latter not seldom allowed himself to indulge at the expense of beauty were little to SCHUBERT's taste, we may infer from the following passage from his diary, written on the day of SALIERI's jubilee, after the pupils of the latter had arranged a performance of their compositions: "It must be delightful and refreshing for the artist to hear in the compositions of his pupils simple nature with its expression, free from all oddity, such as is now dominant with most musicians and for which we have to thank one of our greatest German artists almost exclusively; from that oddity that mingles without distinction the tragic with the comic, the agreeable with the repulsive, the

---

[*] In German a song of this kind is called *durchcomponirt*, *i. e.*, composed throughout, as explained above. In the absence of a better substitute for the German word we may use the expression "wholly-composed", the antithesis of which would be "strophic", or "strophically-composed".

Translator.

heroic with yelling, the holiest with the harlequin, that sets men crazy instead of melting them in love, provokes them to laughter instead of lifting them up to God." In spite of this divergent tendency of SCHUBERT's, in regard of the ideal of beauty, from that of BEETHOVEN, who is doubtless here meant* by "one of our greatest German artists", he was filled with admiration for the older master, to whose imposing artist-personality he had from childhood — SCHUBERT was born in 1797, nearly a generation after BEETHOVEN — looked up with a mixed feeling of love and awe. And when he died (1828) of nervous fever at the age of hardly thirty-two years, his last words were: "BEETHOVEN is not here"; which led his relatives to bury him in the vicinity of his great predecessor. More than all this, however, SCHUBERT's compositions for orchestral and chamber-music attest his intellectual fellowship with BEETHOVEN, for, not to deny his inclination to elegance and pure beauty, he was able to approach the master who was unattainable in these departments more closely than any one of his contemporaries or successors.

And yet it was not granted to SCHUBERT to find for a single one of his larger instrumental works, except his E-flat trio, recognition during his life-time. The short duration of his artistic career, the immediate and overpowering nearness of BEETHOVEN, whose works took up just then the entire and eager attention of the more seriously active friends of music, while on the other hand the ROSSINI opera held the great public in its fetters, — these are the reasons why SCHUBERT did not find the merited universal appreciation until considerable time after his death. It was only as song-composer that he was celebrated by his contemporaries, especially after his intimate friend the singer VOGL, of the Royal Opera, Vienna, had introduced to the public his "Erl-king" in the year 1821 — not till five full years after it had been composed! This song made SCHUBERT's name known throughout all Germany, yet even then the demand for other songs of his was in no proportion to his productive power. Scarcely the

---

* SCHUBERT may here have had in view the A-major symphony with its sublime *allegretto* and its wantonly blustering *finale*; or also that passage in the finale of the F-major symphony No. 8, where the amiable trifling in *pianissimo* in C-major is unexpectedly interrupted by a *fortissimo* D-flat in all the instruments.

sixth part of those songs of SCHUBERT that are now known were published during his life-time, although he did not write one that did not bear the stamp of genius, even allowing that the richness of his fancy occasionally led him beyond artistic limits and that the choice of his texts was not always happy.* The song-composers who came after him, MENDELSSOHN, SCHUMANN and ROBERT FRANZ, proceeded more critically in many respects; besides, the incomparably richer development of the lyric poetry of their time enabled them to improve the species in certain directions. But neither the polished form of the MENDELSSOHN song nor the depth of thought of that of SCHUMANN can outweigh the unaffected power and inexhaustible melodiousness of the SCHUBERT song. ROBERT FRANZ alone, in whose songs an unusual artistic formative power is combined with the purest naturalness of feeling, seems called to make up fully for SCHUBERT's loss, and may even now, though still living, be designated his lawful heir.

The peculiarity and significance of the FRANZ song consist primarily in its affinity to the older German folk-song and the protestant choral derived from the same source. With the latter especially FRANZ familiarized himself from his youth up, and in uninterrupted diligent intercourse with the works of HANDEL and BACH, particularly with the chorals of the latter, he acquired for his own constructive work that quiet strength that preserved him from the romantic unrest dominating the world during the years of his development. Just as the protestant choral, with the harmonic richness conditionated by its melody was employed by the masters last mentioned for the grandest contrapuntal creations, so too FRANZ's *melody* step by step contains a latent harmony and may therefore be called in the strictest sense polyphonic. It is to the influence of the old German song and the compositions of BACH and HANDEL that FRANZ's treatment of *harmony* also may be traced. For, while adhering in the main to the modern tonal system — the major and the minor scale — yet in many of his songs, especially those whose texts are of the popular

---

* This especially at the beginning of his career as song-composer. Afterwards he showed partiality for GOETHE's lyric poems, yet the poet does not appear to have reciprocated his partiality, for, though he had frequent occasion to hear those songs of SCHUBERT well executed, he makes no mention of the composer's name in any of his writings.

order, he goes back to the old church-modes and makes use of their characteristic tone-material. Thus he has as it were rediscovered for modern music this almost forgotten tone-world and herewith brought to the former an extremely rich and significant element of expression. *Rhythm* is with FRANZ, in accordance with the intimate blending of tone with language aimed at and attained by him, of uncommon variety, yet utterly without affectation. The pianoforte accompaniment also is, for all its importance, never an impediment to the rhythmical flow of the vocal part: it illustrates the cantilena not from without only, but sprouts forth from it with inner necessity, and is in the same organic relationship to it as that by which the accompaniment in FRANZ's edition of BACH's and HANDEL's vocal works is distinguished from the purely chordal treatment* of the figured bass-part. In concentrating his entire strength upon song-composition FRANZ was actuated by a correct perception of his decidedly lyrically and contemplatively disposed nature. The latter also exercised a determinative influence upon the manner in which he conceives and treats the *poetic matter of his songs*, toning town the excesses of passionate moods and reducing them to measurable quietness. In this respect likewise he approaches the ancient German lyric muse; for though "world-woe", as the characteristic mark of all modern lyric poetry, finds expression in his melodies, yet it appears free from every uncouth distortion or morbid self-contemplation, rather a pure and true expression of the deep yearning after the ideal that penetrates every human heart.

Like lyric, so also dramatic music attained under the influence of romantic poetry to a new stage of development. It is true that the opera had through GLUCK and MOZART been so enriched musically that any increase of its possessions in this regard could hardly be thought of. But on the other hand, from the side of the poetic contents and the form of the libretto the need of an improvement of this art-species also began to be felt in proportion as romanticism in poetry gained in importance. For the rise

---

* That is, the mere translation of the figured basses into the corresponding harmonics or chords, after the old manner before accompaniments were written out in full. The old method had of course its disadvantages — for the accompaniment itself; but at least it implied that the accompanist should be a *harmonist*, not merely an executant.   *Translator.*

and development of *romantic opera* Germany proved to be a specially favorable soil, by reason of the inclination and ability inherent in the German character to go to the bottom of things, to listen intelligently to the revelations of nature, and to fly on wings of fancy to the remotest times and regions. Moreover the feeling of nationality that in consequence of the War of Deliverance had broken out among the majority of Germans could be better satisfied with romantic opera than with the previous one, because the former was forced by its subject-matter, mostly taken from German popular tradition, to the cultivation of a national coloring of both poetry and music. Here indeed there was imminent danger, for both arts, of losing the artistic equilibrium in the conflict of the world of fancy with reality, and of giving up too much to the subjective-imaginary. Yet it was precisely music that was enabled to settle this dispute by sharp delineation of characters and faithful picturing of situations, and having been required to enlarge its technical means in order to the attainment of this end, it has to thank romantic opera for an enrichment which subsequently turned to its advantage in other departments also.

Ludwig Spohr (1784—1859), Carl Maria von Weber (1786—1826) and Heinrich Marschner (1795—1861) became the musical interpreters of the moods and inclinations above mentioned as slumbering in the German nation. Spohr, superior as musician to both his rivals, as his numerous and solid instrumental works attest, shows himself in the dramatic line as the weakest of them. His tendency to hyper-sentimentality and elegiac pathos prevented him from consistently working out his characters, and it is only where there is question of describing situations and incidents analogous to his very limited sensationary method, as, *e. g.*, in his "Jessonda" (first performed in 1823), that he is able to produce dramatic as well as musical effect. Far superior to him as dramatic composer is Marschner, a master in the representation of the unearthly and demoniacal (*e. g.*, in "The Vampyre", 1828), as also in the delineation of plebeian and comic characters. In this Marschner is not equalled even by Weber; with the latter it was the universality of artistic talent that, without prejudice to his German nature, gave his music so quickening a power that it aroused enthusiastic admiration not only in the composer's native land, but — which was not the case with either SPOHR's or MARSCHNER's music — far beyond the boundaries of Germany.

Not only the artistic achievements of WEBER, but his life-experiences also demand our full sympathy. A wandering life from childhood on, necessitated by the circumstances of his father, a theatre-director, and the consequent unsystematic instruction, could not detract from the ardor of his artistic endeavors, any more than did his successes as pianoforte-virtuoso in his boyhood and adolescence. While yet in his twenty-fourth year, after he had written his first opera "Das Waldmädchen" (The forest Maiden, afterwards re-constructed as "Sylvana"), and filled a music-directorship, he received instruction from Abbé VOGLER, in order to make up by serious studies in composition for what he had lost before. He attained to the full development of his power in 1813 as music-director, at a theatre in Prague, yet without finding here perfect satisfaction, especially because his strong national feeling found on the non-German soil only insufficient nourishment. Berlin, the starting-point of the efforts of German patriotism, which WEBER had artistically glorified in his settings of KÖRNER's Songs of Freedom, "Leier und Schwert", — Berlin would have been the sphere of his activity quite in accordance with his wishes, if it had not been that here, just at this time — strange anachronism! — the musical herald of the conquered French emperor, SPONTINI, had by direction of FREDERICK WILLIAM III. entered upon the management of operatic affairs in general. A call to the newly-established German opera in Dresden could only partially indemnify the master for the failure of his Berlin plans, for, among other annoyances, he had to put up with many hindrances to his exertions through the rivalry of the Italian opera, still in high favor at court, and of its music-director MORLACCHI. This explains why he did not succeed even in bringing out his masterpiece "Der Freischütz" at the place of his personal activity. It was Berlin that through the first performance of "Der Freischütz" (1821) paid the German master a debt of honor, so to speak, and at the same time became the theatre of one of the most brilliant triumphs of German music. For German opera had not only, with this work, entered into its full rights, it had also gained a victory over Italian opera in no wise less important than the one achieved forty years before in Paris by GLUCK, for henceforth in the Prussian capital the foreign musical supremacy was destroyed, the success of the "Freischütz" had put an end to the belief in SPONTINI's musical infallibility.

In the "Freischütz", which depicts in tones the true love of chaste and sincere young hearts, and at the same time the demoniac powers by which man is ensnared, all this on the subsoil of romantic forest-life, WEBER created a work of art whose popularity can hardly at any time be excelled.

The farther course of the romantic tendency exhibited by German music shows us two musicians who are through their creations so near to the present, and have found in our day so complete a recognition, that it will suffice here to characterize their attitude towards musical development in general. FELIX MENDELSSOHN-BARTHOLDY (1809—1847) and ROBERT SCHUMANN (1810—1856) are the chief representatives of that school whose aim is the progressive cultivation of instrumental music on the basis of BEETHOVEN's legacy. To surpass BEETHOVEN in productions of this kind we have already declared to be impossible, yet it was not denied to the two masters above named to extend in certain directions the expressional sphere of instrumental music. Thus MENDELSSOHN excelled, in faithfully painting nature by tones, not BEETHOVEN only but WEBER also, as *e. g.* in his overture "Meeresstille und glückliche Fahrt" (Calm sea and happy voyage), and even undertook to bring to view rural pictures entirely by orchestral means, as in the overture "Die Hebriden" (The Hebrides) and the symphonies in *A*-major and *a*-minor, which have a double right to their surnames "the Italian" and "the Scotch", since they mirror in their music, besides the national character, also the landscape-scenery of these countries, as personally observed by the composer on his travels. In mastering large, broadly developed forms SCHUMANN proves to be the more highly gifted, surpassing MENDELSSOHN in depth of thought also, so that with his symphonies and chamber-compositions, perfect in form and full of the charm of romanticism, he may stand at the head of the representatives of post-beethovenian instrumental music.

We may not, however, look for the centre of gravity of his achievements, nor of MENDELSSOHN's either, in orchestral music or in the large forms generally. The thoroughly subjective nature

of both artists, which in SCHUMANN's case even led him towards
the end of his career to obstinately wrap himself up in the personal sphere of feeling and thought, induced them to work by
preference in the small and smallest forms, those in which the
transitory moods of the individual man are, so to speak, instantane-
ously photographed into an art-work, as in the song, and still
more in the art-species invented by MENDELSSOHN, the "*Lied ohne
Worte*" (Song without words) for the pianoforte, in which the
composer may follow the momentary inspirations with incomparably greater liberty than in the vocal song, being free from the
restraints of words and prosody. In this species of mood-pictures
both MENDELSSOHN and SCHUMANN have produced important works,
the latter in his "Kinderscenen", "Noveletten", etc.; yet music here
ran the risk of losing itself too much in the individual and of
suffering a loss of its universally available power. MENDELSSOHN's
subjectivity found a salutary counterpoise in his attachment to
BACH and HANDEL (we have already seen, in speaking of his oratorios, how favorably his workmanship was affected by his study
of the works of those masters). SCHUMANN on the other hand
allowed the subjective mood and the romantic longing to have so
boundless a control, especially in his pianoforte-works, that HER-
DER's previously quoted observation (see p. 11) on the danger of
separating instrumental from vocal music here finds confirmation;
for in fact SCHUMANN's pianoforte music not seldom "transplants
us into a realm of obscure ideas, and awakens feelings which in
the torrent of artificial tones without words find no leader." From
what has been said it is self-evident that neither MENDELSSOHN
nor SCHUMANN had special talent for dramatic music, for this
branch is conditionated by the artist's ability to objectivate himself, to bring his own individuality into conformity with the outer
world, and to make his creations appear as if detached from his
person. The fragments left behind by MENDELSSOHN of the opera
"Loreley" cannot fail, despite their great musical value, to strike
the hearer as being adapted for the concert-room, not for the
theatre, and SCHUMANN's opera "Genoveva", which the Leipsic
critic J. C. LOBE not inappropriately called a large wholly-composed* song, could in consequence of a lack of dramatic vigor

---

* See *Note*, p. 143.

lead only a sham existence, after repeated trials at different German theatres.

Not less luxuriantly than in Germany did romanticism develop itself among the French, especially after VICTOR HUGO had in the thirties of our century stepped forward as poetic champion of the romantic ideas. The musical representatives of these ideas, HECTOR BERLIOZ (1803—1869) and FRANZ LISZT (born 1811), can however hardly be accounted French musicians (the latter cannot because of his Hungarian nationality): for as they found in instrumental music the tone-material corresponding to their creative artistic impulse, they were consequently obliged to seek their point of support among the German masters of instrumental composition. With their profound reverence for BEETHOVEN, however, which LISZT especially could attest, having placed his incredible powers as pianoforte-virtuoso at the service of the master, it was difficult for them to avoid the rock on which part of their German art-associates had been shipwrecked, in so far as these had gone on building up on the basis of the Beethovenian instrumental music. Yet both were enabled to escape this danger by entering into a happy alliance with poetry and taking the latter as their pilot on their voyage through the stormy sea of tones. They chose a determinate poetical material as the basis of their instrumental works, that by it they might be stimulated to composition though without restraint upon their freedom, and thus became the creators of the so-called *Program-music*. This path taken by BERLIOZ and more decidedly by LISZT in his "Symphonic poems" has often been designated a false one, and even so resolute a champion of artistic progress as RICHARD WAGNER at first repudiated program-music as "an egotistic endeavor of the separate arts to communicate a purport lying outside of their sphere and unattainable by their own means". Later on, however, he changed his opinion, because — as he says in his monograph "On FRANZ LISZT's symphonic poems" — he had meanwhile come to understand "that program-music does not aim to override speech or the plastic arts and represent things accessible to them only, but rather forms a special kind of union of two independent factors: poetry and music." Granting, now, that this union of audible music with poetry that operates solely in the mind of the hearer is but an extremely loose and imperfect one, and that the coöperation of both arts during the art-enjoyment itself is difficult to prove, yet it cannot be denied that poetry even in this case affords the creative master a prop during the development of his thoughts and leads him to the invention of new forms, while to the hearer it materially facilitates the understanding of the musical art-work.*

The characteristic note of the musical romanticists of France, that union of the art-spirit of diverse nationalities, is seen most plainly in FREDERIC CHOPIN. Born of French-Polish parents in 1809 near Warsaw, and ripened into an artist amid intimate mental intercourse with the German instrumental masters, he could build up on the basis of the sensationary method of three nations blended in him, a tone-realm of his own in which he exercised unlimited sovereignty. The chivalrous feeling and the historic sorrow of the Pole, the easy elegance and gracefulness of the Frenchman, the romantic profundity of the German are united in CHOPIN into a total of such originality that his music, though conceived for the pianoforte solely, has extended its fructifying effects beyond the sphere of that instrument. Few composers have found at the beginning of their career so little recognition as he did, yet he soon succeeded by his own strength in gaining a position far overtopping that of his rivals, and his creative genius took afterwards, despite bodily sufferings, so powerful a flight that he was able at his early death (1849) to bequeath to the musical world a heritage of inexhaustible riches.

The faculty, grounded in the nature of the pianoforte and raised by CHOPIN and LISZT to a surprising height, of embracing

---

* Program-music misses its aim only when it undertakes to represent concrete feelings and determinate incidents, as, *e. g.*, when FROBERGER (17th century) endeavors to describe the adventures of a trip on the Rhine in a pianoforte suite, "in which is represented among other things how one of the party hands the boatman his sword, and in so doing falls into the water", — and KUHNAU, in his "Musical representation of some biblical histories in six sonatas for the pianoforte", pretends to illustrate musically JACOB's deception of Laban. Under this head comes also SEBASTIAN BACH's Capriccio on the departure of his brother, with the "representation of diverse accidents that might happen to him abroad", and finally, BEETHOVEN's "Battle of Vittoria", and his imitation of the singing of birds in the second movement of the "Pastoral" symphony, though this work may for the rest be reckoned as program-music in the best sense of the word.

in itself alone the entire expressional sphere of music, and serving as the organ of the sensations of the individual in their widest extent and independently of every foreign coöperation — this faculty enables us to recognize the preponderance of the pianoforte in modern times over the other instruments, as a phenomenon essentially conditioned by the romanticism of the 19th century, notwithstanding that the origin of modern pianoforte-playing reaches back to the classical epoch of the preceding century. The fathers of modern pianism are MOZART, who had inherited the traditions of J. S. BACH transmitted by EMMANUEL BACH, and MUZIO CLEMENTI born at Rome in 1752, died at London in 1832), who was not behind MOZART in thoroughness, and in elegance of playing even surpassed him. These masters became the heads of two schools, which we may designate as the Vienna school and the London school, and of these it was, strange to say, the former in which virtuosity first gained the upper hand over the strict serious style. MOZART's pupil JOHANN NEPOMUK HUMMEL 1778 —1837, is in fact the representative of the new tendency, which, while thorough, at the same time does not despise brilliancy and dash. In the twenties of our century CARL CZERNY (1791—1857) became the head of the Vienna school, from which thenceforth a great number of virtuosi came, in whose performances was prominently manifested the endeavor to astonish by finger-dexterity at the expense of the musical subject-matter. On the appearance, next, of the three most eminent pupils of CZERNY — FRANZ LISZT (born 1811), SIGISMUND THALBERG 1812—1871) and THEODOR KULLAK (born 1818), pianoforte-playing again took for its aim the solution of higher art-problems. Of these, LISZT and KULLAK especially have leaned upon BEETHOVEN, entering into the spirit of this master, who stands alone also in his treatment of the pianoforte, and awakening the understanding of his artistic revelations that was still slumbering in more distant circles, while THALBERG, by the cultivation of a particular side of pianoforte technics — *cantabile* playing — enlarged the expressional capacity of the instrument in accordance with the new demands.

The London school of CLEMENTI was continued by his pupil J. B. CRAMER 1771—1858), who acquired principally through the study of the works of BACH and HANDEL that mastery in pianoforte composition that we admire in his famous "Studies". Other notable pupils of CLEMENTI are LUDWIG BERGER (1777—1839), MENDELSSOHN's teacher, and JOHN FIELD (1782—1837), famous for his Nocturns, closely akin to those of CHOPIN. — A third school of pianoforte-playing, originated in Prague about the beginning of the century, directed at first by DIONYS WEBER then by TOMASCHEK, found in the pupil of the former, IGNAZ MOSCHELES (1794—1870), its chief representative, who, like C. M. VON WEBER and MENDELSSOHN, took a direction as player and composer in which brilliant technics and intellectual depth prevail throughout. On French soil the artistic feeling for the pianoforte that was formerly so richly developed seems to have disappeared for a considerable time, for among the pianists that excelled there after RAMEAU's death not one of prominent distinction is found. Not till the appointment of LOUIS ADAM as teacher at the Paris Conservatory does French pianoforte-playing begin to lift itself up again, and soon afterward ADAM's pupil, FRIEDRICH KALKBRENNER (1778—1849), could claim the attention of the whole world by his playing and his compositions, although he by no means followed strict artistic maxims, but rather, in union with his younger contemporary, HENRI HERZ, became the author of the shallow drawing-room music that exclusively captivated the great public for several decennaries. Over against them there was however no lack of artists in Paris also that extended the cultivation of pianoforte-playing in the spirit of the classical masters, at their head HENRI BERTINI (1798—1876), basing himself on CLEMENTI's school and honorably known by his "Studies", which in pedagogic value are hardly below those of CRAMER; moreover, ZIMMERMANN and STAMATY, to whom the present French generation of pianists owes its development, ALKAN (senior) and LACOMBE to the former, to the latter SAINT-SAENS and others.

As the spread of pianoforte-playing increased from year to year it was unavoidable that the other instruments should fall by degrees into the background, and that the public interest in them should more and more decrease. Even the violin had to yield up the brilliant position it had held during the second half of the 18th century, especially in Italy, where the schools of CORELLI (Rome), VIVALDI (Venice) and TARTINI (Padua) had fostered classical violin-playing and by means of their pupils propagated it over all Europe. Nevertheless it blossomed anew even in this century in the French violinist-school founded by VIOTTI, a descendant of TARTINI's school, the representatives of which former, RODE, KREUTZER and BAILLOT may claim, as virtuosos and composers, but especially as authors of the celebrated "Méthode de Violon" Paris, 1803, a high rank among the patrons of this instrument. Afterwards Belgium became the theatre of the development of violin-playing, where DE BÉRIOT and his pupil VIEUXTEMPS presided over a school that aimed at the cultivation of brilliant technics, yet without losing sight of the exemplars of classical times. While the Italian violin-school, formerly so influential, had in the meantime lost all importance — for even the genial PAGANINI was unable to exert a fructifying influence on the slumbering productive power of his native country — in Germany a school was called into life by LOUIS SPOHR, that with the same success as the French school of VIOTTI preserved and farther developed the valuable acquisitions of the older Italians. SPOHR's merits with regard to the violin, both as virtuoso and as composer and teacher, transcend those that he gained in regard of romantic opera. In the former capacity he aroused universal admiration side by side with PAGANINI, whom he met in Italy during the winter 1816—17. In his numerous violin compositions the noble and tender feeling predominates throughout that characterizes his dramatic works also, and with it the finest sense of the technical peculiarities of the instrument. As teacher he influenced the whole of violin-playing Germany, in part personally, partly through his excellent "Violin School", published in 1831, finally also through his pupils, of whom his biographer ALEXANDER MALIBRAN names no fewer than one hundred and eighty seven. Among these FERDINAND DAVID distinguished himself by his comprehensive activity at the Leipsic Conservatory, to which he was attached as teacher from its foundation in 1843 till his death in 1873.

Until towards the middle of our century we see musical romanticism expanding itself more and more under the guidance of MENDELSSOHN and SCHUMANN. Then came the eventful year 1848, in which the political and social aims that during the first half of the century were only obscurely perceived, showed themselves in perfect clearness to humanity hungering for progress. MENDELSSOHN was not to survive the movement of that year;

SCHUMANN was most likely externally touched by it as is shown by his "Four marches, 1849", in which he endeavored to represent on the pianoforte the impressions of the martial life about him — meanwhile his art-tendency remained the same, in fact his inclination to romantic dreaminess increased to the point of morbidness. And yet the epoch with its positive acquisitions urged to the setting up of new aims for art also; for, if SOCRATES gives the warning "nowhere to change the laws of music and to introduce no new music-species unless simultaneously with the most important civic regulations",* yet we may maintain on the other hand that so radical a change of "civic regulations", so powerful a revolution as that of the year 1848 necessarily involved a change also of art-aspects and art-needs. To satisfy this desire, to substitute something new for romanticism, which had outlived its time, required a more robust artist-nature than that of MENDELSSOHN and SCHUMANN, or even of their epigones. In RICHARD WAGNER, with whom our musico-historical survey comes to an end, we shall become acquainted with the man who with rare many-sided talent and iron will-power opened new careers to music, and, as is made more plainly manifest from year to year, has by his reformatory labors supplied the need of progress felt not only by his own nation but by the entire cultivated world.

---

* Cited by PLATO in his "Republic".

XII.

RICHARD WAGNER.

The discussion of an artist still living and creating among us* in the same line with the greatest masters of the past is, to be sure, on principle not allowable, because to his contemporaries is denied a general survey of his work, and it must therefore be left to a later time to authentically determine its value.** If

---

* The German original of these lectures was published in 1879. RICHARD WAGNER died on the 13th of February, 1883.   *Translator.*
** Just as we cannot correctly judge the height of a mountain when we are near to it, and it is only at a certain distance that we can notice its proportion to the neighbouring peaks, so too the judgment for or against an extraordinary phenomenon in the art-domain will be erroneous until it can be surveyed in its entire significance, which experience shows us to be impracticable for contemporaries and granted to a succeeding generation only. This by no means new experience, as also the other, that categorical judgments favorable or unfavorable to a new tendency antagonistic to the older one constantly lead only to fruitless party disputes, should not however induce us to remain passive and wait till the new ideas struggling for existence have either conquered or been conquered. We ought rather to use all diligence to appropriate them, to overcome the feeling of strangeness that on superficial acquaintance separates and repels us from them: in this way we shall show fair play to the pioneer artist who offers us the best he has, the richest treasures of his mind, and at the same time form a counterpoise to the great number of those who, chiefly from indolence and dread of what seems strange, disdain these gifts and then are soon ready to condemn the giver. But after we have become intimate with the new art-tendency and have clearly recognized the intention of its representative, we should not withdraw ourselves from his leadership at an arbitrarily determined point; we should rather regard it as an artistic duty to follow the man of whose superior art-insight we have once had proof, even when he strikes out a path differing from his previous one. The so common saying: "I have all respect for So-and-so, but I do not go with him through thick and thin", is at bottom nothing but the ridiculous

nevertheless in RICHARD WAGNER's case we make an exception to the principle according to which history has to do only with what is already accomplished, we are justified herein for many reasons. First, because the movement originated by him has its starting-point in the facts of an artistically glorious past; next, because the ends to which he aspired have through his literary labors been most accurately indicated and made discernible to every one; lastly, because more than a generation is already behind us since he excited universal attention by his artistic creation, so that a survey of this latter is even now to a certain degree practicable. To occupy ourselves in detail with what WAGNER has done as poet, composer and philosopher is of course impracticable in this place, in view of the immense extent of it all, as also of the limited time at our disposal. Nothing more can be done here than to cast a glance at the formation-process of WAGNER's art, and, since the chief moments of his eventful life are in close relation to his artistic development, a short sketch of his career up to the well-known events of the last years will be the best means of attaining our end. For, as GOETHE happily puts it to his friend ZELTER, after affirming his partiality for the study of musical history, "who understands any phenomenon when he is not penetrated by the process of its origination?"

RICHARD WAGNER was born in Leipsic on the 22^d of May, 1813, only four years after MENDELSSOHN and three years after SCHUMANN, accordingly as contemporary of the men beyond whose musical sphere of thought he took, a generation later, so powerful a leap that one should be inclined to imagine a distance of many generations. The cannon's thunder of the battle of the nations, which, announcing Germany's deliverance, was mingled

---

assumption of prescribing to genius the domain of its creative labors, of drawing the lines beyond which it may not go. "When we think we have discovered something wrong in an approved author", says COLERIDGE, "we should first assume that *we* are unable to understand him, until we have fully satisfied ourselves of *his* incapacity." The fate of RICHARD WAGNER's works can leave no doubt that the observance of this rule would have spared the artist many a disheartening experience, and his over-hasty critics many a subsequent mortification. Moreover WAGNER is by no means alone in his experiences: the lot of his "Tannhäuser", "Lohengrin", "Tristan and Isolda", and "Meistersinger" was the same as that of RAMEAU's operas, for instance, each one of which fell through on its first performance because — it was not sufficiently like its predecessor, *i. e.* surpassed it in significance.

with the suckling's first indications of life, the national enthusiasm amid which he received his earliest impressions, can hardly have failed to have an enduring influence on the development of the child's disposition. In his very cradle that love of country must have germinated in him that afterwards proved to be one of the essential traits of Wagner's character, and which neither his clear intelligence of foreign superiority in some points nor the obstinate mistrust he long met with in Germany was ever able to weaken. His artistic predispositions likewise even in tender childhood did not lack nourishment, thanks to the loving stimulation of his step-father, the play-actor Ludwig Geyer, who left nothing undone to compensate the boy for the early loss of his own father. His musical education was, to be sure, not a success, and the instruction in pianoforte-playing had, on account of the pupil's aversion to purely technical study, to be given up after a short time. On the other hand, as pupil of the Kreuzschule at Dresden, whither his family had removed after Geyer's death, he showed a lively interest in ancient languages and antique poetry. The Greek poets especially attracted him, afterwards Shakespeare also, through which latter he was inspired, before attaining adolescence, to his first poetical attempt. This was a grand tragedy, of which the author himself tells us that it occupied him two full years, and in the matter of piling up bloody combats was on a par with any of the dramas of his great model. "Forty two men died in the course of the piece, and at the performance I found myself obliged to let most of them reappear as ghosts, as otherwise I should have had no personages in the last acts."[*]

To this period belong also the first lasting impressions on the youth's musical nature, the occasion of which was a performance of "Der Freischütz", which was enthusiastically received in Dresden as previously in Berlin, in spite of the opposition of the champions of Italian opera, as also of the poets of literature, whose head, Ludwig Tieck, had called "Der Freischütz" "the most unmusical clatter that had ever blustered on the stage". Wagner's admiration of Weber's art and person, which dated from that time, was not diminished in the course of his development, not even when, in Leipsic, after he had returned thither in

---

[*] R. Wagner, Autobiographical sketches, in his collected writings.

consequence of his step-father's death, he had become familiar with BEETHOVEN's music. This acquaintance was by all means calculated to take up the exclusive attention of the fifteen year old youth for some time; the "Egmont" music particularly so affected him that he resolved to make music his profession, being stimulated to this chiefly by the desire of bringing his tragedies before the public with similar musical accompaniments. That he was the man to compose such music one day, and that he also need not fear the difficulties of the study requisite for it, was for him virtually a matter of course; but this was not the opinion of his relatives, to whom it appeared a serious matter that the young enthusiast should exchange the already adopted profession of poet for another. A union of the poetical and musical callings, in view of the opinions dominant at their time to some extent even now, and after the practice of a century had, in spite of all efforts to the contrary, as it were sanctioned the division of this work between two persons, necessarily appeared to them a fantastic and aimless undertaking.*

WAGNER too had to acknowledge the necessity of his devoting himself primarily to music exclusively, in order to attain the end held out before him, and accordingly he began, after completing the scientific course (first at the Leipsic "Nicolaischule", afterwards at the University). to give himself up to the study of counterpoint with all diligence. Aided in this by the preceptor of the "Thomasschule". WEINLIG, and in farther attempts at composition by HEINRICH DORN, at that time music-director at the Leipsic theatre, he was able as early as 1833 to come before the

---

* The yearning for the re-union of the poet and the musician in one person appears since the downfall of antique culture to have never entirely died out, for we repeatedly find it expressed by artistically inclined natures. Thus, FREDERICK THE GREAT writes to the electoral princess MARIA ANTONIA of Saxony, who had sent him two operas written and composed by her: "You give an example to composers, who, in order to succeed well, should all be *poets at the same time*." And LESUEUR, music-director at the church of Notre Dame, Paris, complains, thus, in an essay published 1787, of the restrictions put upon the catholic church-composer: "Oh! if it were only permitted to the musician to write the *words!* What could he not do!" Examples of similar vain wishes might be multiplied indefinitely; all the fewer for this reason appear the musicians who contrary to custom have regarded it as an artistic duty to write their text themselves.

public as composer, to wit, with a symphony, which was performed at one of the "Gewandhaus" concerts, as also with a concert-overture, played during the same season. He approached still more nearly the practical side of his calling on a journey undertaken soon after to WÜRZBURG, where his brother ALBERT was engaged as singer and play-actor and he himself temporarily took part in the theatrical performances as chorus-leader. Here he also composed his first dramatic work, a three-act romantic opera "The Fairies", the text of which he himself had written after GOZZI's "La donna serpente." He was very anxious to have this maiden work performed, after he had returned to his native city: yet new obstacles were constantly arising to cause delay, and as a turn in the direction of WAGNER's taste had occurred at this very time, after he had through the agency of the celebrated singer Madame SCHRÖDER-DEVRIENT recognized the charm and the merit of Italian and French opera, he lost all interest in his own opera and threw away the advantage of a public performance. Literary activity now indemnified him for the success denied him for the time being as creative artist. An essay written under the influence of AUBER's opera "Masaniello" exhibits him to us as the inexorable adversary of one-sidedness and routine, in which character he afterwards provoked a no less bitter opposition. "We certainly have", he maintains, "a department of music that is peculiarly our own, and that is instrumental music; but a German opera we have not, for the same reason that we have likewise no national drama. We are much too intellectual and much too learned to create warm human forms. ... I have of course no desire that French and Italian music should crowd out our own, but we ought to recognize the true in both and beware of all selfish hypocrisy. — We ought to breathe anew out of the rubbish that threatens to stifle us, to get rid of a good lot of affected counterpoint and at last become human."

The position of theatrical music-director at Magdeburg, upon which WAGNER entered in the autumn of the following year (1834), afforded him ample opportunity to satisfy his many-sided art-needs as above expressed. The motley change in the opera-repertory of a German city-theatre, the daily rehearsal and direction of German, Italian and French operas, together with the experiences thus gained, helped him to bear cheerfully the burdens of his new calling and kept up his courage, though he often had to acknowledge that his efforts to elevate the theatre would be unsuccessful, owing to its petty surroundings. Meanwhile a second opera also had been finished: "Das Liebesverbot", founded on SHAKESPEARE's "Measure for measure", the music of which shows an incomparably greater freedom than that of "The Fairies", which was strongly influenced by WEBER. This work was put on the stage in the winter of 1836, but the circumstances of its performance were so little favorable that, with the exception of some tolerably well executed scenes, it produced no effect, while the author realized on this occasion more deeply than ever the dark side of his calling and recognized the impossibility of achieving anything artistically advantageous with the means at the disposal of a city-theatre of smaller rank. He determined therefore to adapt his next great work from the very outset to a stage of the first rank, without troubling himself where or when he should find the latter. With this view he made the sketch of a grand tragic opera in five acts: "*Rienzi, the last of the Tribunes*", and so planned it as to render it impossible to produce this opera — at least, for the first time — at a theatre of limited resources. For the present WAGNER continued of course to be assigned to stages of subordinate rank, having to act as theatrical music-director in 1836 in *Königsberg* and in the following year in *Riga*. That he did not find artistic satisfaction in either of these cities was no more than what he should have expected after his previous experiences, and as he had moreover to struggle with material cares he formed the resolution — in his circumstances a romantic one — of removing to Paris, to arrange there, if possible, for the production of the meantime finished "Rienzi" at the Grand Opera.

In the summer of 1839 this plan had been matured: the journey was entered upon in a sailing-vessel bound for London — "The voyage" — writes WAGNER — "lasted three weeks and a half, and was full of disasters. Three times we suffered from a most violent tempest and the captain was once obliged to run into a Norwegian harbor. The passage through the Norwegian headlands made a wonderful impression on my imagination: the legend of the "Flying Dutchman", as I heard it confirmed by the sailors, took on in me a determinate and peculiar color, that only the sea-adventures I had had could impart to it." After a short stay in London WAGNER betook himself to Paris, where he arrived in the autumn of the same year, rich in hopes but with greatly reduced finances. Being entirely without letters of introduction he had no one but MEYERBEER to go to, having made his acquaintance on his journey, in Boulogne, where the latter had most cordially promised his assistance. But neither his own energy nor the efforts of his influential colleague could guard the sanguine artist against those disappointments that were necessarily involved in the enormous competition of skilled labor in the French capital. During the very first winter he was forced to the conviction that in the state of things in Paris, regulated by the laws of fashion and of speculation, his ideal tendency would with difficulty ever find appreciation. The extreme poverty that sometimes forced him to lay aside all independent art-labor, that he might gain a subsistence by literary work for the "Gazette Musicale" and by opera-arrangements, even for the cornet, increased his bitterness against his surroundings. This feeling of his found its utterance in the *Overture* — composed during this winter — *to* GOETHE's "*Faust*", the motto of which indicates the mood that was fermenting in the artist's interior and was transferred to the composition:

> "The god who thron'd within my breast resides,
> Deep in my inmost soul can stir the springs;
> With sovereign sway my energies he guides.
> But hath no power to move external things;
> And thus my very being I deplore,
> Death ardently desire, and life abhor."

We pass over the unhappy period from the beginning of 1840, the date of the Faust-overture,* till the spring of 1842, when WAGNER, without having gained a single success, but for that all the richer in experience, turned his back upon the French capital.

---

* This work is worthy of note for two reasons: first, as being the first of WAGNER's works to give to the great public evidence of vitality; second, because here, in the midst of so much that is gloomy, we recognize the energetic nature of the artist, which does not allow itself to be overwhelmed, after the manner of the earlier romanticists, by the miseries of life and the world-woe, but courageously enters into the fight with the powers of darkness and at the end comes off victorious.

The news that his operas "Rienzi" and the long finished "*The Flying Dutchman*" had been accepted for performance, the former in Dresden the latter in Berlin, had thrown a cheerful light upon his ever darkening prospects, and at the same time powerfully kindled in him the yearning for his native country. He arrived in Dresden just in time to superintend the rehearsals of the "Rienzi" and to be witness of the enthusiastic applause with which the public, in spite of high-wrought expectations, received the work on its first performance (Oct. 20, 1842). As the composer was appointed music-director at the opera-house the very next year and thus made sure of a subsistence, one should naturally think that the time of trial was over for him. Had he only been content to remain standing at the stage of development now reached, to follow as poet-composer in future, as he had already followed in his "Rienzi", the prototypes of French grand opera, and to tread conscientiously the path indicated by his predecessors — his artist-career would presumably have elapsed in undisturbed peace. But nothing of all this occurred. At the very appearance of "The Flying Dutchman" (Berlin, January 1844) the friends of his art-tendency, who had expected a kind of music like that of "Rienzi", felt for the greater part dissatisfied; but still greater and more general was the disappointment when in 1845 the "Tannhäuser" had its first performance. The effect of this opera even on the Dresden public was, despite WAGNER's personal relations to it, one of such surprise that the artist once more had to bear the whole weight of the feeling of isolation. Moreover, as director he had in the very first days of his official duties in many ways offended his superiors as well as his subordinates by his want of consideration in combating the abuses inseparable from operatic affairs. Under these circumstances he was convinced that even under the most highly favorable conditions, such as the Dresden court-theatre was well able to offer, a realization, though but approximate, of his artistic ideals was entirely out of the question.

If we put ourselves in the place of the artist, whose ill humor had passed over into perfect discouragement after he been obliged to give up even the hope of bringing out his "Lohengrin",[*] which

---

[*] It was not till 1850 that the "Lohengrin" was performed, through the

meantime (1847) had been finished, we can scarcely wonder that the storm-and-stress year 1848 found him in the ranks of the discontented. As regards his active participation in the reform-movement of that year he kept himself, it is true, strictly within the limits of his calling, and restricted himself to laying before the Saxon minister of public worship and education a "Plan for the organisation of a German national theatre", whose chief aim was the change of the Dresden court-theatre into a national theatre, and its support by the state and assignment to the ministry of instruction, in accordance with its destination as institute for popular culture.* Nevertheless, with his warm and always unreservedly expressed interest in social and political questions generally it was inevitable that he too should become involved in the disturbances of May, 1849, and figure, after the reaction had set in, with his name on the list of the suspected. Fortunately he realized the danger of his position early enough to enable him to take flight. A writ of arrest sent after him and renewed as late as 1853, commanding the German authorities "to seize WAGNER, RICHARD, one of the most prominent adherents of the Destructives,** in the event of meeting him, and to hand him over to the royal city court at Dresden", must have removed from his mind every doubt as to the dangers from which his flight had delivered him.

By way of Paris, where he found the soil for his endeavors not more favorable this time than at his first sojourn, WAGNER arrived at Zurich, and being thus a second time snatched away from the native soil so indispensable for his practical art-labors, he now felt the urgent desire to attain by the way of theory a thorough clearing up of his ideas, to give himself and them that

---

agency and under the direction of FRANZ LISZT, at Weimar, where the latter had a year before taken the position of court-music-director. WAGNER himself had to wait eleven years longer before it was granted to him (during his residence in Vienna in 1861) to hear his work for the first time.

* This very important work, which however at that time utterly failed of success, is found in WAGNER's collected writings, Vol. II.

** "A name given by their political opponents to men who call themselves radical reformers", is the definition of the original German word "Umsturzpartei" (literally, "party of subversion") given in FLÜGEL's German and English Dictionary. *Translator.*

were striving with him a detailed account of the reasons and aims of his reformatory activity. Here, far from musical occupation and without any opportunity whatsoever to manifest himself as executive artist, he began a *literary activity* that as complement of his musico-poetic activity is hardly of less importance than this latter. In his first publication "Art and Revolution", which appeared in 1849, WAGNER expresses his dissatisfaction with the modern practice of art, whose moral aim he pronounces the acquisition of money, its esthetic pretence the amusement of the *blasés*. He hopes for an improvement of this state of things solely through a return to the ancient art-conditions, the essence of which he declares to be man's joy in himself and in nature, in opposition to Christianity, which preaches discomfort and the refraining from all spontaneity, in order to break forth from the condition of intellectual oppression.* Especially the Theatre, in which all arts combine to form the highest art-work, the drama, is to be released from a servitude to which at the present day all men are subjected, viz: industry.** "If industry is no longer our master, but our servant, we shall make the aim of life the delight of existence and strive to render our children, by means of education, capable of and fitted for the most effective enjoyment of this delight. Education, starting from the exercise of strength, from the fostering of personal beauty, will, out of undisturbed love for the child, and out of joy in the increase of its beauty, become a purely artistic one, and every man will in one respect or another be in truth an artist."

In a second, larger work — "The art-work of the future" (1850) — we find these principles farther carried out in an art-reformatory sense. WAGNER here indicates the people as the conditionating power for the art-work, and man — in conformity with the teaching of LUDWIG FEUERBACH, to whom the book is inscribed — as his own god and superior to nature. For this man that art alone is suitable that, as the only true one, arises

---

* FRANZ BRENDEL, one of the earliest champions of WAGNER's theories, in his "Music of the present" justly calls attention to the fact that WAGNER, in announcing a great "revolution of humanity", overlooked the social side of the christian doctrines, through which this revolution was already called into life.

** Less euphemistically, "working for one's living".   *Translator.*

from the combination of all our art-genera. The individual arts, that hitherto quarreled and separately strove for precedence, ought to draw near to each other in reciprocal love and modesty and take each its proper rank, in order at length to unite, in the drama, for the joint art-work, the art-work of the future. — Still more sharply does WAGNER define his aim in a third work, — "Opera and Drama" (1851). Here he sets out from the maxim that modern opera, as art-species, is an error, since in it a means of expression — music — is made the *end*, and on the other hand the true end — the drama — becomes a *means*. Only by unity of poetry and music can the music-drama attain immediate effect. But to obtain this unity each of these two arts must sacrifice the conventional peculiarities developed in them in the course of time: speech must again lay hold of the musical elements (see page 9) that were lost in the progress of its development and concern itself exclusively with material that, like the Greek myth and the German national legend, addresses itself to sensuous perception. The music — more correctly, the melody, as its essence — must not exist for its own sake but spring naturally from the expressively delivered language, and be in uninterrupted connection with it as also with the action represented on the stage.

In his philosophical investigations WAGNER followed at first the doctrines of L. FEUERBACH, afterwards those of ARTHUR SCHOPENHAUER, whose theory of life is already partially expressed in his poems written before his acquaintance with SCHOPENHAUER's philosophy, but afterwards was fully accepted by him and genially applied for determining the nature of his art. SCHOPENHAUER, in his principal work "The World as Will and Idea", which, appearing in 1819, was for decennaries long almost unnoticed, denotes the world surrounding us as a *phenomenon* (*Vorstellung, i. e.*, representation or idea formed by ourselves, to which he confronts the *Will* as the *real*. His conception of the latter is however to be taken in a sense far transcending the commonly accepted one, as he understands by it not only the conscious desire, but also the unconscious impulse, even down to the forces manifesting themselves in organic nature. The will, in SCHOPENHAUER's view, is the essence of the world and the kernel of every phenomenon, the permanent in the constant alternation of rise and decay of external things, hence synonymous with the "Ideas" of the Platonic philosophy, and with the "thing in itself" of that of KANT. But whereas the "ideas" in PLATO's sense can be imagined only notionally, and KANT holds the "thing in itself" to be unknowable, it is possible for us, according to SCHOPENHAUER, to comprehend the substance of things, in as much as perception breaks loose from its original subjection to our will and no longer regards things in their relations to it. By this means the perceiving subject ceases to be a merely individual one, and rests in fixed contemplation of the object presented out of its connection with any others and becomes identified with it.*

Now this kind of perception is the origin of art, which repeats the eternal ideas comprehended through pure contemplation, the essential and permanent of all the phenomena of the world. In the art-work we recognize the *archetype*, of which the individuals making their appearance are only *likenesses*. Art alone is capable of temporarily freeing us from the torment of life, which latter is according to SCHOPENHAUER a constant suffering.** Life

---

* "If", — says SCHOPENHAUER in his work above named — "lifted up by the power of the spirit we let go the usual way of looking at things, and cease to follow up radically, by the clue of the formations of the sentence, only their interrelations, whose final aim is always the relation to the individual will, thus considering no longer the Where, the When, the Why and the Wherefore, but only the What; and do not allow abstract thought, the conceptions of reason, the consciousness to be captivated, but instead of all this yield the whole power of our intellect to contemplation, sink ourselves entirely in it and allow our whole consciousness to be filled with the quiet contemplation of the natural object happening to be present, be it a landscape, a tree, a rock, a building or anything whatsoever; utterly losing ourselves in this object, *i. e*, precisely forgetting our *individuum* our will and continuing to exist only as mere subject, as clear mirror of the object, so that it is as if the object alone existed, without any one to perceive it, and thus we can no longer separate the contemplator from the contemplation, but both have become One, the whole consciousness being entirely filled and possessed by one single perceptible image; when, I say, in this way the object has stepped out of all relation to anything outside of it, the subject out of all relation to the will, then that which is thus perceived is no longer the individual thing as such; it is, rather, the *Idea*, the eternal Form."

** In his Ethics SCHOPENHAUER indicates as man's highest duty the suppression — not of life itself, but — of the desire to live, by means of asceticism. Here his doctrine agrees on the one hand with that of the Buddhists concerning the removal of suffering by quitting the checkered world of life Sansara and entering into unconsciousness Nirvana, and on the other hand

is never beautiful (says he in another place), but the images of life alone are, to wit, in the transfiguring mirror of art or of poesy. The essential denotement of the nature of the artist is his ability to see constantly the general in the particular, to recognize in individuals the ideas expressing themselves in them. "What we call the quickening of genius, the hour of inspiration, the moment of enthusiasm, is nothing else than the liberation of the intellect, when the latter, temporarily freed from its subjection to the will, no longer sinks into inactivity or exhaustion, but, for a short time, entirely alone, of its own accord is active. It is then of the greatest purity and becomes a clear mirror of the world; for, entirely separated from its origin, the will, it is now the very world as idea concentrated in *one* consciousness" (*ibid.*).

WAGNER, in his monograph "BEETHOVEN"* (written in 1870 for the celebration of the centenary of the master's birthday) starts out from the above doctrine for attaining musico-philosophical results of the greatest importance. SCHOPENHAUER had already ascribed to music a nature entirely different from plastic and poetic art, and recognized in it not merely a *copy* of the idea of the world but *this very idea itself*. As for the phenomena of the visible world outside of us, their character in the abstract most clearly speaks to us out of the works of plastic art, "the proper element of which, consequently, is the employment of the illusive semblance of the world, spread out before us by the agency of light, for the manifestation, by virtue of a highly thoughtful play-

---

with the ascetic elements in Christianity. The same theory of life forms also the basis of WAGNER's grand and touching poem "Tristan and Isolda", in which we find repeatedly expressed not only SCHOPENHAUER's view of the world as a phenomenon of our own creation; but also the yearning to fly from the deceptive light of day to the twilight of unconsciousness, — as, for instance, in the words:†

"Blissful beams our eyes are binding,
"Abashed is earth with radiance blinding;
"Lit by the daylight's dazzling lie,
"Undaunted by falsehoods which we defy,
Thou'rt my world, thine am I."

* This work has been translated into English with the author's express permission and approbation, by Mr. ALBERT R. PARSONS. New York, G. SCHIRMER, 1883.

†) The translation given is Corder's.   (*Translator.*)

ing with that semblance, of the Idea which it veils. * * * * But the *semblance of things*, to the contemplation of which we devote ourselves during moments of æsthetical perception free from Will, always remains the effective element here. * * * * Our consciousness which, even in gazing at a semblance, alone enables us to grasp the Idea which is manifested by it, may at last feel impelled to exclaim, with Faust:

"A wondrous show! but ah! a show alone!
"Where shall I grasp thee, infinite nature, where?"

The most certain of answers to this cry is given by *music*. The outer world speaks to us with such incomparable intelligibility here, because, by virtue of the effect of sounds, it communicates to us through hearing precisely what we call out to it from the depths of our soul. The Object of the tone that is heard coincides immediately with the Subject of the emitted tone; we understand without any intermediation through conceptions what is said to us by the cry for help, or of mourning or joy, which we hear, and answer it at once in the corresponding sense * * * No illusion, as in the semblance of light, to the effect that the fundamental nature of the world external to us is not completely identical with our own essential nature, is possible here, by which the gulf that to the sight seems to exist at once vanishes."*

The antagonism that the appearance of the first named writings of WAGNER called forth was especially violent, for the reason that their author had attacked together with the existing opera its representatives also, some of whom were still living, and had acted, it was charged (as too often happens in like cases), from personal motives in uttering his opinions. But even among those who did not doubt of the purity of his artistic intention WAGNER was unable, owing to the roughness with which his theory confronted the temporarily ruling one, to find for the time being more than slight appreciation. This state of things was not improved when the artist courageously followed up his theories by deeds, and in his music-drama "Tristan and Isolda" finished in 1859) consummated with most perfect consistency the break with the previous opera-form. Nay, the verbal and tonal language of

* "BEETHOVEN". A. R. PARSONS' translation, pp. 26, 27, 28.

the "Tristan", so utterly divergent from the operas of his predecessors and even from his own "Tannhäuser" and "Lohengrin" which had meanwhile become known and liked, estranged from him even a part of those art-friends who had till then been his supporters. Moreover it was reckoned certain that the difficulties of performance were insuperable, after the efforts made at Carlsruhe and Vienna to produce the work had been of no avail. Under these circumstances Wagner resolved in the year 1859 to appeal a third time to the susceptibility of the Parisian public; but this time also he was to be deceived in his faith in the French art-insight that had so unequivocally been displayed at the appearance of GLUCK. For the public, although to a certain extent familiarized with the new music-tendency through a series of brilliant and artistically successful concerts in the Théâtre Italien at the beginning of 1860). felt, at the subsequent performances of the "Tannhäuser" (in March, 1861), so annoyed in its artistic routine and expressed its displeasure so recklessly — even a critic so experienced and a musician so devoted to progress as BERLIOZ joined on this occasion in the almost universal sentence of condemnation! — that the author had no resource but to withdraw his score after the third performance.

Again poorer by one expectation WAGNER left Paris, and, the interdict resting upon him from 1849 having meanwhile been raised, turned to Germany, where the number of the friends of his art had increased from year to year and sympathy for him had in consequence of his Parisian experience been greatly intensified. It was of course not yet his fortune to find a permanent abode for his work. Then occurred the event so momentous for his artist-career, the accession to the throne of LUDWIG II. of Bavaria. This prince, filled with love for WAGNER's art from boyhood. hesitated not a moment to call the master to him at Munich (1864), and to place absolutely at his disposition the rich musical resources that the royal residence afforded. WAGNER obeyed the call, and the proximate consequences of his emigration were the establishment of a music-school according to his plan, as also the performance of "Tristan and Isolda" (1865) with the co-operation of the SCHNORRS, husband and wife, in the title-roles, and under the direction of HANS VON BÜLOW, when it was proved that this work, formerly accounted impracticable, requires only the entire devotion of the artists engaged in it to attain its effect without fail.

We have thus arrived at the third period of the master's life — that is, if the second must be dated from the appearance of his "Rienzi" — and have accordingly reached the limits imposed at the outset upon this short recital. The subsequent principal events of his career have been as it were personally lived through with him by the art-friends even of the latest generation, and scarcely need to be specially brought into prominence. How WAGNER saw his restless activity so hindered even in Munich that he was obliged to leave the city even at the end of 1865; how he then finished* his "Meistersinger von Nürnberg" in the rural solitude of his villa Tribschen near Lucerne, and with the first performance of this work in Munich in 1868, despite all the counter-currents working there met with a triumph that put all his previous successes in the shade: finally, how he conceived at the beginning of our decennium the idea of the Bayreuth Festival-plays, and spite of the boldness of this plan found so warm an interest in it that as early as 1872 (on the 22^{d} of May, the artist's fifty-ninth birth-day) the corner-stone of the theatre to be built for this purpose could be laid — all this lives still fresh in the memory of contemporaries. So too the most significant event in WAGNER's life, the bringing about (in 1876) of the *Festival-plays at Bayreuth*, up to the last day considered by doubters an impossibility, and their inauguration by the representation of the *Nibelungen-trilogy*, composed to that end.

If there is any indemnity at all for the sufferings and disappointments that are never lacking to the artist who is in advance of his time, it must on these memorable days have been granted to RICHARD WAGNER in unusually rich measure. For here he was able to attain to the certainty that the German nation, though represented at *Bayreuth* of course by a small fraction only, attached itself to him in full confidence and had learned to appreciate his exertions in behalf of German art. And many a one of the festival guests, in so far as he did not allow his

---

* According to the date of origin the "Meistersinger" comes between "Tannhäuser" and "Lohengrin", for the poem was sketched by WAGNER as early as 1845, while he was at Marienbad.

feeling of susceptibility to be disturbed by the external defects that were unavoidable by reason of the novelty of the undertaking, but dispassionately gave himself up to the solemn frame of mind induced by the seclusion of the place and the concurrence of thousands of like mind — many a one of them must have felt during those days the full significance of HERDER's prophetic words uttered (with reference to GLUCK) almost a century before: "the progress of the century will lead us to a man, who, despising the frippery of wordless tones, perceived the necessity of an intimate connection of human feeling and of the myth itself with his tones. From that imperial height on which the ordinary musician boasts that poetry *serves* his art, *he* stepped down and made his tones only serve the words of feeling, the action itself. He has emulators: *and perhaps some one will soon outstrip him in zeal, overthrowing the whole shop of slashed and mangled opera-jingle and erecting an Odeon, a consistently lyric edifice, in which Poetry, Music, Action and Decoration unite in one.*"

APPENDIX.

TABLE

for memorizing certain dates of musico-historical importance.

Although it is not to be expected of the reader that he should memorize the dates occurring in this short recital (to say nothing of those found in more detailed works on music-history), yet the retention of some few dates, round about which the remaining facts may group themselves, may be considered an indispensable condition of successful study. For facilitating this I have in the following Table placed opposite to the musico-historical dates certain well-known epochs of general history, the latter having been chosen solely on mnemotechnic grounds, although, in conformity with the character of the book, reciprocal relationships between the development of music and that of general history were kept in sight as far as possible.

Antiquity and the Middle Age.

753. **Rome** founded by Romulus and Remus.
600. **Solon**, law-giver of Athens, an opponent of dramatic representations.
490. Victory of the Greeks over the Persians at **Marathon**.

776. Beginning of the **Olympic games** and of the Olympiad-era.
600. **Thespis** brings about the transition from the Bacchus-festivals (Dionysia) to Tragedy.
472. **Attic Tragedy** reaches its climax in **Aeschylus**. Performance of "The Persians".

429. Death of **Pericles**.

404. End of the **Peloponnesian War**; the leadership in Greece passes over from Athens to Sparta.

338. Battle of **Chæronea**. Downfall of Grecian liberty.

336. **Alexander the Great** accedes to the throne.

Separation, with **Euripides**, of the calling of the poet from that of the musician.

405. Palmy days of **Attic Comedy**. Performance of "The Frogs", by **Aristophanes**. Development of the **Sophistic Philosophy**. Development of **Oratory**. **Demosthenes** died 322.

Aristotle died 322. His pupil, the music-theorist **Aristoxenos**.

A. D.

68. Death of the emperor **Nero**.

333. **Constantine the Great** proclaims Christianity the state religion.

375. Beginning of the **Migration of Nations**.

526. Death of **Theodoric the Great**, King of the Ostrogoths in Italy.

622. Establishment of Islamism by **Mahomet**.

814. Death of **Charlemagne**.

1077. **Emperor Henry IV.** does penance at **Canossa** before Pope **Gregory VII**.

1270. End of the **Crusades**.

1305—1377. Residence of the Popes in **Avignon**.

1453. Conquest of **Constantinople** by the **Turks**.

67. **Nero's art-journeys** in Italy and Greece.

314. **Pope Sylvester** founds in Rome the first singing-school.

367. The **Council of Laodicea** forbids congregational singing.

386. Archbishop **Ambrose** introduces into the church of Milan the chant named after him.

524. Death of **Boethius**, last philosopher and music-theorist of antiquity at the court of Theodoric.

604. Death of Pope **Gregory the Great**, founder of the Gregorian Chant.

840—930. **Hucbald**. First attempts at polyphonic music **Organum** or **Diaphony**.

1024. Pope John IX. **Guido of Arezzo's** method of vocal instruction and improvement of music-notation.

1200. **Franco of Cologne**, oldest writer on mensural music.

1380. The Netherlander **William Dufay**, member of the papal choir at Rome.

1476. The Netherlander **Tinctoris** publishes the first music-lexicon: "Terminorum musicæ diffinitorium".

APPENDIX.

1492. Discovery of America by Columbus.

1517. Martin Luther posts 95 theses against Indulgences on the door of the Cathedral at Wittemberg.

1563. Close of the Council of Trent.

1572. Massacre of St. Bartholomew.

1600. Marriage of Henry IV. of France and Maria de' Medici at Florence.

1490. Adrian Willaert, founder of the Venetian school, born at Bruges.

1521. Death of Josquin des Près. Netherlandic counterpoint at the climax of its development.

1565. Performance of Palestrina's three 6-voiced masses dedicated to Philip II., among them the "Missa Papæ Marcelli".

1570. Orlando Lasso, music-director at Munich, finishes his Penitential Psalms.

1600. First performance of the music-drama Euridice by Rinuccini, music by Peri, and of the sacred music-drama "La rappresentazione di anima e di corpo", by Cavaliere.

Modern Times.

1618—1648. The Thirty Years' War.

1673.* Passage of the Test-act, in England, under Charles II.

1685. Repeal of the Edict of Nantes.

1704.** Battle of Blenheim.

1725. Death of Peter the Great. Russia received among the European Powers.

1627. First appearance of opera in Germany. (Performance of Rinuccini's "Dafne" with music by Schütz in Torgau.)

1637. Establishment of the first public opera-house, the Teatro Cassiano at Venice.

1672. Lulli acquires the supreme direction of operatic affairs in France.

1685. Bach and Handel born.

1703. Handel begins his labors for the opera at Hamburg.

1725. Death of Alessandro Scarlatti. The Neapolitan school founded by him obtains supremacy throughout Europe.

1729. First performance of Bach's Matthew-Passion at Leipsic.

---

* I have taken the liberty of substituting here for the "Battle of Fehrbellin", with its date, 1675, an event of more interest to the English-speaking reader. (*Translator.*)

** Historical event substituted see above Note for that given in the original. (*Translator.*)

1740. Accession of **Frederick the Great** to the Prussian throne.

1740. **Handel** closes his operatic career and devotes himself to **Oratorio**.

1756. Beginning of the **Seven Year's War**.

1756. **Mozart** born.

1775.* Battles of **Lexington** and of **Bunker Hill**.

1774. First performance of **Gluck's** "**Iphigenia in Aulis**", at Paris.

1795.* **Partition of Poland** by Russia, Prussia and Austria.

1795. Establishment of the Paris "**Conservatoire de musique et de déclamation.**"

1805. Battle of **Austerlitz**. Napoleon I. in Vienna.

1805. First performance of **Beethoven's** "**Fidelio**" at Vienna.

1809. Battle of **Wagram**.

1809. Death of **Joseph Haydn** at Vienna.

1813. Battle of the **Nations** near Leipsic.

1813. **Richard Wagner** born. First performance of **Rossini's** "**Tancredi**", at Venice.

1821. Death of **Napoleon I.** at St. Helena.

1821. First performance of **Weber's** "**Der Freischütz**", at Berlin.

* Historical event substituted (see Note, p. 177) for that given in the original. (*Translator.*)

INDEX.

Accentus ecclesiasticus, 105, 106 111.
Adam de la Hale, 41.
Adam, Louis, 154.
Æolian Scale, 19.
Æschylus, 8.
Alkan, 154.
All Fools' Day Fools' Festival, 105.
Amati, 132.
Ambrose, Archbishop, 20.
Ambrosian Chant, 22.
Ancient disuse of final minor Triad, 65.
Ancient Greek music, tone-genera of, 19.
Ancient Modes, the, reduced to two, 53.
Animuccia, 107.
Anti-bouffonites, 83.
Antiphonary, 24.
Antiquity, the music of, 1.
Arabians, the, influence of on culture, 26.
Aristoxenus, "the Musician", 12.
Ars organandi, 28.
Artistic (Italian) singing, 71.
Art-song, 142.
Ass's Festival, 105.
Auber, 91.
Authentic Mode, 21.
Azione sacra 107.

Bach, C. P. Emanuel, 127. 137.
Bach, J. Sebastian, 83. 94. 113. 124, 135.
Baïf, 75.
Baillot, 155.
Bardi, Giovanni, 61.
Basso continuo, 108.
Bassoon, 132.
Bassus generalis, 108.
Bass-viola, 131.
Bayreuth, festival-play 172.
Beak-flute flute à bec, 132.

Beauchamp, 78.
Beethoven, Louis van, 101. 137. 140.
Bellini, 73.
Berger, Ludwig, 154.
Berlioz, Hector, 151. 171.
Bernhard, Christoph, 94.
Bernhard, the German, 124.
Bertini, Henri, 154.
Boccaccio, 52.
Boethius, 16, 17.
Boieldieu, 91.
Bombard, 132.
Bouffonites and anti-bouffonites, 83.
Bow-instruments, 131.
Bülow, Hans von, 171.
Buxtehude, 124.
Byrd, William, 117.

Caccini, Giulio, 61.
Caldara, 70, 109.
Cambert, Robert, 77. 117.
Camerata, of Florence, 61.
Campra, 81.
Canon, 48.
Cantabile pianoforte playing, 153.
Canzone, 134.
Carissimi, Giacomo, 68. 109.
Cassiodorus, 16.
Cavaliere, Emilio dal, 108.
Cavalli, 67.
Cembalo, 125.
Chamber-cantata, 109.
Chamber-music style, 68.
Champeron, 78.
Charlemagne, 23.
Cherubini, 90.
Chinese, music-system of the, 3.
Chopin, Frédéric, 152.
Chorus, origin of the, 64.

12*

Chromatic element in music, the, 64.
Church-music, 109. — in the 18th century, 72. — at Hamburg, 94.
Clarinet, 132.
Classic, Classical, 59.
Clavicembalo, 125.
Clavichord, 125. 126.
Clement of Alexandria forbids the chromatic tone-series, 16.
Clementi, Muzio, 153.
Complete system of ancient Greek music, 18.
Composer, function of the, in the Middle Age, and in Luther's time, 58.
Confrèrie de la Passion, 105.
Congregational singing, forbidden by the Council of Laodicea, 20. — promoted by Luther, 56.
Conservatoire de musique, etc., of Paris, 90.
Contest of singers at the Wartburg, 42.
Contrabasso, 132.
Contrapunto a mente, 47.
Corelli, 135. 154.
Cornet, 132.
Council of Laodicea forbids congregational singing, 20.
Council of Trent on church-music, 58.
Counterpoint, 37. 47. 60.
Couperin, François, 127.
Cousser (Kusser), 96.
Cramer, J. B., 153.
Cristofali (Christofori), 128.
Cross-flute (Flauto traverso), 132.
Crotta, 131.
Crusades, the, influence of on Western musical culture and poetry, 40.
Cuzzoni, 71.
Cyclical instrumental forms, 135.
Cyprian de Rore, 64.
Czerny, Carl, 153.

Dance, the, originally accompanied vocally, 133.
Dance of Death (Danse Macabre), 106.
Dante, 52.
Dauvergne, 84.
David, Ferdinand, 155.
de Bériot, 155.
Diaphony, 28.
Diruta, Girolamo, 136.
Discant, 37. 45.

Dissonance, 51. 66.
Dittersdorf, C. D. von, 100.
Doles, 120.
Donizetti, 73.
Doric tetrachord, 17.
Dorn, Heinrich, 160.
Double choir, origin of the, 64.
Dowland, John, 117.
Dramatic music, influenced by Romanticism, 146. — of Mendelssohn and Schumann, 150.
Dufay, Guillaume, 47.
Dulcimer, 128.
Duni, 85.
Dunstable, 116.
Durante, Francesco, 70. 72.

Earliest Christian times, music of the, 15.
East-Indians, their music-theory, 2.
Eccard, Johannes, 110.
Ecclesiastical Modes, 21.
Eginhard, 23.
Egyptians, the, 4. 6.
Ekkehard, 24.
Elizabeth, Queen of England, 116.
England, musical position of in the Middle age, 115.
Enharmonic tone-genus, 20.
Equal temperament, 82.
Equilibrium in ancient-times between tone and speech, abolished through
Euripides, 10.
Esthetics, 139.

Faburden (Faux-bourdon), 46.
Fagotto, 132.
Festival-play at Bayreuth, 172.
Fiddle, 131.
Fides, 131.
Fidula, 131.
Field, John, 154.
Fifths, parallel, earliest prohibition of, 37.
Figella, 131.
Figured bass, 109.
Flauto traverso (Cross-flute), 132.
Flute, 123. 132. 133.
Flûte à bec (Beak-flute), 132.
Folk-song (Volkslied), 45. 49. 56. 130. 142.
Fools' Festival (All Fools' day), 105.

INDEX. 181

Forkel opposes Gluck, 89.
Form of the Scarlatti overture, 69 (note).
Four-voiced vocal music, earliest example of, 46.
Franco of Cologne, 36. 38.
Franz, Robert, 145.
French opera, 75.
Frescobaldi, Girolamo, 124. 134.
Froberger, 124.
Fugue, 48.
Fux, Johann Joseph, 70.

Gabrieli, Andrea, 66.
Gabrieli, Giovanni, 66. 134.
Gafor, Franchinus, 46.
Galilei, Vincenzo, 61.
German idealism, 137.
German Opera, 92. 148.
Germany, first opera-performance in, 92.
Germany, Italian opera in, 70.
Gesualdo, Carlo, 68.
Gibbons, Orlando, 117.
Gluck, Christopher von, 86. 97. 99.
Gluckites and Piccinites, 87.
Gossec, 90.
Goudimel, Claudio, 59.
Graun, Carl Heinrich, 71. 120.
Greek music-system, 17.
Greek tragedy, origin of, 7.
Greeks, music of the, 7.
Gregorian chant, 22.
Gregorian tones, 21.
Gregory the Great, 20.
Grétry, 85.
Guarneri, 132.
Guido d'Arezzo, 32.
Guidonian Hand, 34.

Haendel (Handel), G. F., 70, 96. 112. 113. 115. 117.
Hamburg, church music at, 94. — German opera at, 93. 96.
Hand, the Guidonian, 34.
Harmony, ancient meaning of, 29.
Harpsichord, 125.
Hasler, Hans Leo, 110.
Hasse, Faustina, 71.
Hasse, Johann Adolph, 70. 71. 120.
Haydn, Joseph, 98.
Hebenstreit, Pantaleon, 128.
Herz, Henri, 154.

Hexachord system, 34.
Hilary, Pope, 20.
Hiller, Johann Adam, 98. 130.
Homophonic style of pianoforte playing, 136.
Hucbald (Ubaldus), 28.
Hummel, Johann Nepomuk, 153.
Hyporchema, 133.

Idealism, German, as affecting German instrumental music, 137.
"Improperia" (Reproaches), 59.
Instrumental forms, cyclical, 135.
Instrumental music, 11. 122.
Instrumental style, 133.
Instruments with keys and bows, 123.
Invention of the pianoforte, 129.
Invention of music-printing, 51.
Ionian Scale, 19.
Italian opera, 63. 70.
Jewish musical culture, 6.
Johannes de Muris, 37.
Jomelli, 72.
Jongleurs, 41.
Josquin des Près, 50.

Kalkbrenner, 154.
Kant, Immanuel, 138.
Kauer, Ferdinand, 100.
Kayser, Christoph, 99.
Keiser, Reinhard, 94. 96. 112.
Key, idea of, in antiquity, 3.
King of the violins, 45.
Kreutzer, 155.
Kuhnau, Johann, 136.
Kullak, Theodor, 153.
Kusser (Cousser), 96.

Lacombe, 154.
Laodicea, Council of, 20.
Lassus (Lasso), Orlando, 110.
Laudi spirituali, 107.
Leibnitz, 138.
Leipsic, German opera at, 98.
Leo, Leonardo, 70.
Lied ohne Worte, 150.
Liszt, Franz, 151. 153. 164.
Lotti, 109.
Lulli, Giovanni Battista, 78.
Lute, 129.
Luther, Martin, 54. 56.

Lydian tetrachord, 17.
Lyric poetry, 11. 112.

Madrigal, 60. 68.
Manelli, 67.
Marcello, Benedetto, 109.
Marchand, Louis. 127.
Marchettus of Padua, 37.
Marenzio, Luca, 60.
Marius, 129.
Marschner, Heinrich, 147.
Marseillaise, La, 90.
Martin, Vincenzo, 72.
Master-singers, 42.
Master-song, German, end of, 44.
Mattheson, 91. 112. 127.
Mazarin, Cardinal, 76.
Medieval notation of mensural music, 36.
Méhul, 90.
Mendelssohn-Bartholdy, Felix, 120. 145. 149.
Merulo, Claudio, 121. 134.
Meyerbeer, 91. 163.
Minnegesang (Minnesong), 42.
Minnesinger, 42.
Minstrels (Jongleurs), 41.
Minuet, 137.
Missa Papæ Marcelli, 59.
Mixtures (organ), 124.
Mode, 21.
Modes, ecclesiastical, 21.
Modes, the ancient, reduced to two, 83.
Monochord, 125.
Monody, first appearance of, 61.
Monsigny, 85.
Monteverde, Claudio, 66. 134.
Morales, 107.
Morlacchi, 118.
Morley, Thomas, 117.
Moscheles, Ignaz, 154.
Mozart, 97. 99. 100. 140. 153.
Müller, Wenzel, 100.
Murer, Bernhard, 124.
Music, dramatic, 116.
Music of the early Christians, 15.
Music of the Greeks, 7.
Musical culture, Jewish, 6.
Musical development of the Egyptians, 4.
Musical elements of speech, 9.
Musical temperament, 65.

Music-notation, Hucbald's attempted reform of, 31.
Music-notation, improved by Guido d'Arezzo, 32.
Music-system of the Chinese, 3.
Music-system of the Greeks, 17.
Music-printing, 51.
Music-theory, 64. 82.

Neri, Filippo, 107.
Nero, Roman emperor, 13.
Netherlanders, musical sovereignty of the, 40.
Netherlandic counterpoint, 48.
Neumes, 31.
Northern nations, as cultivators of instrumental music, 27.
Notation, 31. 32.
Notkers, the two, 24.

Oboe, 132.
Oeckenheim, 49.
Octave-species, 17.
Octave-species, reduced to two, 19.
Olympus, 4.
Onomato-poetic words, 9.
Opera, beginnings of, 62.
Opera, French, 75.
Opera-academies, 78.
Opéra-Comique, 84.
Opera, German, 96. 148.
Opera-house, the first, 67.
Opera, Italian, 63. 70.
Operetta (Song-play, Singspiel), 97.
Oratorio, 104. 107—110. 115.
Oratorio-chorus, 119.
Orchestral symphony, 69. 137. 139.
Organ, 123.
Organating (ars organandi), 28. 45.
Organum, 28. 29. 30.
Organ-pedals, 124.
Origin of scale-names, *Ut*, *Re*, *Mi*, etc., 32.
Ottaviano dei Petrucci, 51.
Overture, Scarlatti's, 69 *note*.

Pachelbel, 121.
Paisiello, 72.
Palestrina (Pier Luigi), 58. 60. 107.
Pan's pipes, 122.
Parallel octaves and fifths, 37.
Paris Conservatory, 90.

INDEX.

Partita, 135.
Pasquini, 124.
Passion, 101. 110—112. 114. 120.
Passion-play, 106.
Paumann (Paulmann, Conrad, 124. 129.
Pergolese, 72.
Peri, Jacopo, 61.
Perrin, Abbé, 76. 78. 79.
Petrarca, 52.
Petrus and Romanus, 24.
Philidor, 85.
Philosophy, Sophistic, 10. 12.
Phrygian tetrachord, 17.
Pianoforte, 126. 129. 136. 152.
Piccini, 70. 72.
Piccinites and Gluckites, 87.
Pier Luigi Palestrina, 58. 60.
Pistocchi, 71.
Plagal Mode, 21.
Poet, in antiquity, 9.
Poetry, lyric, 11. 112.
Polyphonic music, 26. 28.
Porpora, 70. 118.
Prætorius, Michael, 123. 127.
Program-music, 151. 152.
Psaltery, 125.
Purcell, Henry, 117.
Pythagoras, 12. 65.
Pythagorean third, 65.

Quanz, Johann Joachim, 133.

Rameau, Jean Philippe, 80. 127.
Rebec, 131.
Recitative (stile rappresentativo), 61.
Recitativo arioso, 111.
Reduction of ancient modes, 83.
Reduction of the seven octave-species, 19.
Reformation (Luther's) and the Renascence, 54.
Reichardt, Johann Friedrich, 98. 142.
Reinken, Johann Adam, 91. 124.
"Reproaches" (Improperia), 59.
Re-union of poet and musician in one person, Note, 160.
Rinuccini, 61.
"Robin and Marian", 42.
Rode, 155.
Roi des violons, 45.
Roland de Lattre Orlando Lasso', 110.

Romans, the ancient, a native art not developed among them, 12.
Romantic, 141.
Romanticism, 141.
Romanticists of the 19th century, 141. 151.
Rossini, 72.
Rota (Rotte', 131.
Rouget de Lisle, 90.
Rousseau, Jean Jacques, 85. 89.
Rupff, Conrad, 57.

Sachs, Hans, 44. 92.
Sacred music-drama, 109.
Saint-Saens, 151.
Sakadas, 12.
Salieri, 101.
Sarette, 90.
Sarti, 72.
Sax, Adolph, 133.
Scarlatti, Alessandro, 67. 69.
Scarlatti, Domenico, 70. 136.
Scarlatti overture, 69.
Scheidt, Samuel, 124.
Schelble, 120.
Schenck, Johann, 100.
Scherzo, 137.
Scholastic philosophy, 37.
Schopenhauer, 107.
Schröder-Devrient, 161.
Schröter, 129.
Schubert, Franz, 143.
Schumann, Robert, 145. 149. 150.
Schütz, Heinrich, 93. 106. 110. 111.
Sebastiani, 112.
Senesino, 71.
Sequence, 24.
Shawm, 132.
Silbermann, 129.
Singing, artistic, 71.
Solmisation (Sol-faing), 34.
Solo song, first introduced, 61.
Sonata, 134. 135. 136.
Song-form, Note, 133.
Song-play 'Singspiel', 98.
Sophistic philosophy, 10. 12.
Sourdéac, Marquis de, 78.
Spinet, 126.
"Spiritual song-booklet", 57.
Spohr, Ludwig, 147. 155.
Spontini, 91. 148.
Stamaty, 154.

Steffani, Agostino, 68.
Stein, Johann Andreas, 129.
St. Gall, monastery of, 23.
Stile rappresentativo (recitative), 61.
Stradivari, 132.
String-instruments, 122.
Strozzi, 76.
Suite, 135.
Sylvester, Pope, founds the first singing schools, 20.
Symphony, the modern orchestral, 69. 137. 139.
Syncopation, 47.

Tablature, 43. 129.
Tartini, 154.
Telemann, 94. 97. 112.
Temperament, musical, 65. 82.
Tenor, original meaning of, 46.
Tetrachord, 17.
Thalberg, Sigismond, 153.
Theile, 95.
Theodoric, Emperor, 16.
Theorbo, 129.
Theory of music, enriched by Rameau, 82.
Thespis, 8.
Thibaut of Navarre, 41.
Thomas, Ambroise, 90.
Tinctoris, 116.
Toccata, 134.
Tomaschek, 154.
Tone-genera of ancient Greek music, 19.
Tripartite measure in the Middle Age, 36.
Tritone, 35.
Trouvères (Troubadours), 41.
Tutilo, the monk, 25.

Ubaldus (Hucbald), 28.
Umlauf, Ignaz, 99.

"Ut queant laxis" (Hymn), 32.
Ut, Re, Mi, Fa, etc., 32.

Verdi, Giuseppe, 74.
Viadana, Ludovico, 108.
Vielle, 131.
Vieuxtemps, 155.
Vioel, 131.
Viol, 131.
Viola, 131. 132.
Viola da braccia, 131.
Viola da gamba, 131.
Violin, 132.
Violin-making, 132.
Violoncello, 132.
Viotti, 155.
Virginal, 126.
Vittoria, 107.
Vivaldi, 135, 154.
Vocalmusic, four-voiced, earliest example of, 46.
Volkslied (Folk-song), 45.

Wagner, Richard, 156. 157.
Walther, Johann, 57.
Wartburg, contest of singers on the, 42.
Weber, Carl Maria von, 147.
Weber, Dionys, 154.
Weinlig, 160.
Western music-culture and poetry affected by the Crusades, 40.
Wholly-composed song, (*Note*) 143.
Willaert, Adrian, 63.
William of Machaud, 46.
William of Poitiers, 41.
Wind-instruments, 122. 131. 133.
Wulston, his description of an organ, 123.

Zarlino, Gioseffo, 64. 65.
Zelter, C. F., 142.
Zimmermann, 154.

www.ingramcontent.com/pod-product-compliance
Lightning Source LLC
Chambersburg PA
CBHW032142160426
43197CB00008B/750